LUFTWAFFE

A PICTORIAL HISTORY

LUFTWAFFE

A Pictorial History

Eric Mombeek

Acknowledgements

First published in 1997 by
The Crowood Press Ltd
Ramsbury, Marlborough
Wiltshire SN8 2HR

© Eric Mombeek 1997

This impression 1998

**British Library Cataloguing in
Publication Data**

A catalogue record for this book is
available from the British Library.

ISBN 1 86126 093 8

Typeset by M Rules
Printed and bound in Great Britain
by Butler & Tanner Ltd, Frome, Somerset

This work would not have been possible without the help of many people who were
unstinting with their time, patiently helping me with long correspondence or taking
time to meet me. Many researchers did not hesitate to open their own archives and help
me. I want to especially thank Jean-Louis, Jean-Pierre, Marco, Didier and Peter for their
great help.

The photographs come from the following archives:

Wolf Abler, Dan Antoniu, Hans Autenrieth, Dorothea Bacsila, Martin Bauer, Wilhelm
Becker, Günther Behling, Wolfgang Betz, Hans Biederbick, Karl-Heinz Böttner, Gaston
Botquin, Ehrard Braune, Heinrich Brunsmann, Fernand Capon, Jean-Pierre Chantrain,
Roland Charlier, Remy Chuinard, Jim Crow, Yves Empain, Eppler, Marco Fernandez-
Sommerau, Hannes Forke, Richard Franz, Walter Giese, Adolf Glunz, Graphopresse,
Alfred Grislawski, Manfred Griehl, Hannibal Gude, Hans-Georg Güthenke, Family of
Hans *Assi* Hahn, Erich Hartmann, Alfred Heckmann, Karl Helber, Martin Hempfling,
Friedhelm Henning, Heinrich Heuser, Dr Carl Hofner, Rudolf Hübl, Gerhard Huth, Yves
Huard, Wolfdieter Huy, IHCA (Instituto de Historia y Cultura Aeronautica, Madrid),
Dragustin Ivanic, Aloïs Job, Erich Jung, August Graf von Kageneck, Karl Kern, Rüdiger
Kirchmayr, Kurt Klöpper, Karl-Heinz Koch, Friederich Körner, Wolfgang Kretschmer,
Kroll, Elias-Paul Kühlein, Josef Lackmann, Ernst Laube, Knut Maesel, John Manhro,
Walter Matthiesen, Julius Meimberg, Jochen Menke, Hans Meyer, Karl Meyer, August
Michalski, Family of Erich Mix, Eric Mombeek, Hellmuth Müller, Alfred Nitsch, Gerd
Noschinsky, Hans Obert, Reinhold Omert, Karl Opitz via A. Ragatzu, Photos PK, Photo
de Presse Française, Alessandro Ragatzu, Heinz Richards, Aloïs Riebl, Jean-Louis Roba,
Heinrich von Podewils, Heinrich Sannemann, Ernst Scheufele, Karl-Fritz Schlossstein,
Family of Reinhold Schmetzer, Otto Schmid, Gottfried Schmidt, August Schneider,
Günther Scholz, Leo Schuhmacher, Peter Schulz, Franz Selinger, Franz Stadler, Otto
Stahlheber, Gerhard Stiemer, Hennig Strümpell, Peter Taghon, Erwin Teske, Pierre
Tiquet, Family of Günther Troebs, US Air Force, US National Archives, Jean-Pierre
Van Mol, Jean Verrycken, Frieder Voigt, Walter Waldenberger, Hans-Gerd Wennekers,
Anton Wöffen, Hans Wolf, Wolfgang Wollenweber, Werner Zirus

To all of them, my greatest gratitude.

Contents

CHAPTER ONE

Rebirth of the Luftwaffe

I joined in 1931 as a Fahnenjunker of 18 years in my Grandfather's regiment and I quickly volunteered to become a pilot. It was a dream and I had not much hope of reaching this goal: the Treaty of Versailles forbade Germany to have an Air Force. Nevertheless, we knew that a Luftwaffe was being recreated secretly. In spite of some eye problems (that I could more or less hide), I was accepted in the DLV (Deutsche Luftsportverband) at Cottbus where I came to know personally the great Udet, the ace of WW I. I learned to fly in a plane of his design. I then flew the Heinkel Kadett, Stieglitz and F-34 Junkers. Even if my unit was apolitical, we viewed Hitler with a degree of hope: he was the only man who could save Germany from her miserable situation. But we were very suspicious of the SA troops.

I asked to become a fighter pilot and was then posted to Schleißheim where I met Generals Ritter von Schleich and Milch. I was very well trained on several types of aircraft at Faßberg, such as the Stösser, and finally on our first fighter aircraft, the He 51, again at Schleißheim. My training as a fighter pilot finished in 1934, at the same moment as when the new Luftwaffe was officially raised. I was naturally posted to a newly forming fighter squadron. My unit was the famous JG Richthofen, first based at Döberitz, and shortly after in Bernburg. I had the task of building its third Gruppe as adjutant to the famed Bruno Loerzer, a WW I ace awarded with the Pour le Mérite Cross, like his comrade Göring. We received a lot of pilots, later to become well-known aces in WW II, such as Galland, Hraback and Brüstellin.

(Lt. Hennig 'Piefke' Strümpell)

Right: JG 135 was formed in 1936. In March 1937, I./JG 135 equipped with He 51s and Ar 68s, moved from the Stuttgart area to Bad Aibling near Rosenheim to become the sole operational fighter Gruppe for all Bavaria. The pilot of He 51 D-IPTI (which flew with the undercarriage spats removed) fell victim to spongy soil, performing what German flyers call a *Fliegerdenkmal* (monument to the aviator). Two years later, the Gruppe became I./JG 51.

Above: He 72 Kadetts of *Jagdverband Bernburg* (a unit tracing its origins to JG 132, the Luftwaffe's first fighting squadron) are carefully laid out in a hangar at Bernburg in early 1937. At that time German aircraft did not carry military markings and were still painted in civilian colours: with 'D' (the international marking for Germany) on the fuselage and the wings, as well as the Swastika cross with white circle and red stripe on the tail.

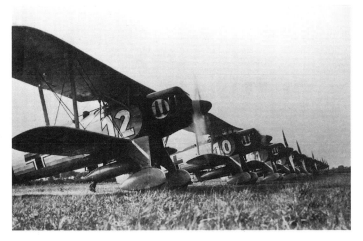

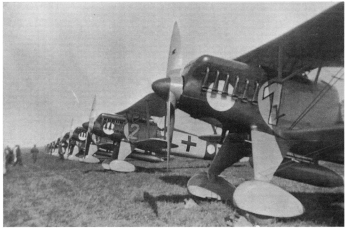

Above: **A line of He 51s of JG 132 on Döberitz airfield (near Berlin) in 1937. This formation originated in the famous *Reklamestaffel*, a secret military unit disguised as a civilian organization to avoid the restrictions of the Treaty of Versailles. This unit is the backbone of the future fighter force, and will give birth to the renowned JG 2, the *Richthofen* Geschwader.**

Above: **These He 51Bs of I./JG 137 were photographed at Bernburg in 1937. The white circle on the cowling and on the fuselage band indicate that these machines belong to the third Staffel of the Gruppe. As with nearly all fighter Gruppen, this unit originated from JG 132. It later became I./ZG 2 and then I./JG 3.**

Above: **In the late 1930s, the most common Luftwaffe bomber type is the He 111. Four of the first pattern of He 111B are aligned here in Insterburg. The code '71' indicates that they belong to KG 157 (in fact they are from the Ist Gruppe). In 1939 this unit will be renamed KG 27 *Boelcke*. Note the clean lines of the fuselage and the two-tone camouflage pattern.**

Left: **Inspired by tests carried out by foreign air forces (Poland, France etc), the Luftwaffe further develop and perfect the concept of dive bombing, principally with the Ju 87. The first model of this aircraft (Ju 87A) that will soon be known under the generic name of *Stuka* (Sturzkampfflugzeug) seems rather lumpish with its thick landing gear legs. Nevertheless, it will revolutionise tactical air warfare.**

CHAPTER TWO

Spanish Civil War

In 1931/32, I was a Sportflieger (sports flyer) but joined the Kriegsmarine in 1934 as, at that time, it was easier to enter that arm than the Luftwaffe, which was still a little nucleus. I met there the future ace and NATO general Johannes Steinhoff who was at that time a warrant officer. Always hoping to fly again, I was not long in asking for a transfer to the new Luftwaffe. In my blue Navy uniform, I went to Salzwedel to begin my training which would be shorter than for my comrades. Indeed, I already had the civilian A-2 licence (light aircraft and aerobatics). In March 1937, I was transferred to a fighter squadron (I./JG 135) at Bad Aibling. At the beginning of 1939, fighter pilots were asked to go to Spain. Nearly all the unmarried pilots were ready to go there. I wanted myself to take part in the 'Crusade against Communism'. The volunteers were also sure of seeing action and having interesting adventures attractive to young men such as we were. We also had the opportunity to fly the more powerful machines of the time… and last but not least the pay was high! (When I came back to Germany I had 1200 Reichmarks in my bank, which allowed me to buy a fantastic car.)

On 15 February 1938, I was transferred to Bernberg, to a unit which only existed on paper, 10./JG 137. This was in fact a smoke screen for the German intervention in Spain. The 'unit' was led by Oblt. Jürgen Roth, who had already flown a 'tour' in the Spanish Civil War (he was Stk. of 3./J88 in 1936/37). We were given all the information on our future theatre of war.

On 27 March 1938, we went to Berlin, and after that, to Rome in a Ju 52. We remained there two or three days before boarding another Ju 52 to Sevilla. I was posted to Adolf Galland's Staffel near Zaragossa. I was surprised to hear that aerial combat was prohibited. Indeed, our He 51s were outclassed in the air by the more modern Soviet machines and, to avoid high losses, our mission was only to drop bombs or to strafe enemy positions. The Ratas (Polikarpovs) were lighter and a little bit faster, those qualities giving them better manoeuvrability in the Spanish skies . . . until the arrival of the Bf 109C.

The new fighter soon arrived in my unit (2./J88, led by Lt. Günther Lützow, already had Bf 109s) and we could give our 'old' He 51s to the Spanish Air Force. At that time (the end of May 1938) Galland handed over 3.J/88 to Oblt. Werner Mölders (the future greatest ace in Spain with 14 claims in six months). I myself had one claim: a Rata. On 10 September, I left RLM Sonderstab 10 (Legion Condor!) and came back to Germany in a Tante Ju. I was then posted to I./JG 130 established in Jesau.

(Lt. Günther Scholz)

Above: **The Junkers 52/3m was one of the most versatile aircraft used in the Spanish Civil War. Its action in transporting Nationalist troops from Morocco to Spain is well known, and even caused Hitler to suggest that Franco should erect a monument to the glory of the *Tante Ju* ('Auntie Ju').**

The Ju 52 was also converted for use as a stop-gap bomber. Slow and poorly protected, it nevertheless fulfilled a useful role, both in Germany and in Spain, before the arrival of more modern aircraft like the He 111 and Do 17. German Ju 52s were used in Spain as bombers until the end of 1937, when they reverted to their transport role. Four Spanish squadrons were formed in 1936, and they dropped bombs until the end of the war. Some transport Ju 52s were also given to Iberia, which became the national airline after Franco's victory.

The Ju 52 shown here was photographed in mid-1937, and wears the insignia of 2. /K88. Bombs can be seen waiting to be loaded. When 2. /K88 was re-equipped with He 111s, the crews adopted a more stylised insignia closer to the official crest of the Luftwaffe.

Previous page below, and above: The Ju 52s formed a key element of air power in Spain – but they were vulnerable. In order to protect the transports, the Luftwaffe had to send escort fighters. The first fighter planes were He 51s, arriving in 1936, initially under civilian cover. This biplane fighter was the best in the Spanish sky until the delivery of the first Soviet fighters to the Republic. The '2' code on the fuselage identifies the type as an He 51, while '106' is the individual identity of this Legion Condor machine (a total of 126 He 51s were sent to Spain). The 'ace of spades' markings of 4./J88 will be readopted during World War II by JG 53 *Pik-As*.

Above: Heinkel 111Bs arrived in Spain in February 1937, replacing the Ju 52 in the bomber role. They served in K/88, and surprised their opponents with their speed and bomb-load. The Heinkel was given the nickname *Pedro*, and had its baptism of fire on 9 March in an attack on two Republican airfields.

In the fierce battle of Teruel at the end of 1937, one aircraft landed by mistake behind Republican lines and was captured intact. It was shipped to the USSR to be tested and evaluated there.

This *Pedro* is a typical example of an He 111 in 1938. It had such a distinctive shape that the unit gave up on camouflage, instead covering their machines in various artworks. This one has a witch painted on the fin, a Champagne bottle in the black circle on the fuselage, and the normal Nationalist cross in black on the white rudder.

Note the unusual shape of the '25' (the type code for the He 111), the crude position of the dorsal gunner and the exposed seat for the ventral gunner (a very windy position not used in winter!).

(Karl Helber)

Above: A rare bird in Spain! It seems that the Legion Condor had only five Ju 34s in the country. Three of them came with the first batch of German aircraft in 1936, followed by two others in 1937. One of them was used as a personal aircraft by General Queipo de llano. All five served in the Spanish Air Force after the end of the Civil War, the last being retired in the 1950s. This machine is shown in 1938, and has a large insignia (possibly a screaming eagle?) on the side of the fuselage. Note that it is being secured on the ground by two bombs – a common habit in this theatre of war.
(Karl Helber)

Right: Another He 111B with the type's nickname *Pedro* painted on the nose. This one appears to have damage under the nose and on the far propeller spinner. Notice the fuselage marking of a black circle with a bomb in the middle.

Left: During World War II, the Heinkel 59 float plane was mainly operated by the *Seenotstaffeln* in the air-sea rescue role. In Spain, however, they were not used in such a peaceful manner! The first five aircraft arrived at the end of 1936 and were assembled in AS/88 (the maritime reconnaissance unit), and around 20 He 59s eventually served in the Civil War. Loaded with bombs or equipped with heavy machine-guns, they were used aggressively in combat patrols and in attacks on harbours.

Significant successes were the attack on the harbour in Almeria (24/25 May 1937), where the warship *Jaime I* was heavily damaged; the sinking of three ships in Alicante harbour (4 June 1938); and the sinking of four more ships in Barcelona (14/15 September 1938). Used by day or night, the He 59s suffered heavy losses (around seven of them being destroyed in combat). The size of their floats caused Spanish flyers to give them the nickname *Zapatones* (or 'big shoes'). The survivors (around five) were given to the Spanish Navy at the end of the war, and flew until 1946. This particular example is seen in 1938 flying over the base of J88.
(Günther Scholz)

Right: It is often written that the Germans used the Spanish war to test new tactics and technologies, and that the Legion Condor made extensive use of the new Ju 87 *Stuka* dive bomber. But, in reality, the Ju 87 was only tested in very limited numbers. The Ju 87A shown here is one of only three that came to Spain around January 1938. They flew with 11./LG 1 and the Spaniards nicknamed them *Estupidos* ('stupid'). They flew some operational missions but returned to Germany in October 1938. Then came five Ju 87Bs which remained in Spain until the end of the Civil War.

Above: **A Do 17F of A/88. Under the cockpit is a personal marking of a lozenge on a white circle, while the engine cowling sports a red devil's head on a white shield. During World War II, this marking will often be used by reconnaissance units (by 7./LG2 amongst others). Around 15 Do 17Fs flew in Spain, and were eventually transferred to the Nationalist Forces in August 1938.**

Right and above: **The Do 17 arrived in Spain in the autumn of 1938, and the one shown here is a Do 17P of A/88, a reconnaissance unit. In German service the Dornier was nicknamed *Fliegende Bleistift* ('flying pencil') because of its slender fuselage, but the Spaniards called it *Bacalao* after the cod, a fish with similar lines. During the Civil War many personal markings were designed and many would reappear during World War II. This machine was flown by Fw. Martin Hering, who went on to serve in III./KG 53 during the 1940 campaign in Western Europe. He transferred to I.(F)/123, a reconnaissance unit, during the Battle of Britain and was killed on 21 October 1940. This particular machine stayed in Spain, and was finally scrapped in 1952.**

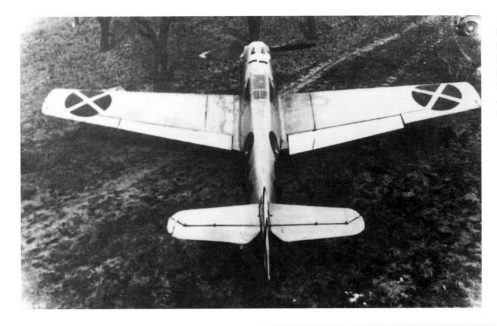

Left and below: **The Bf 109B-1 was the first Messerschmitt fighter to be sent to Spain at the beginning of 1937, after the testing (the future great ace Hannes Trautloft being among the testers) of at least two prototypes. Shown here is Bf 109B-1 '6-15' of Uffz. Otto Polenz, who was captured on 4 December 1937 on the Aragon front. This aircraft was evaluated by a French commission before being shipped to the USSR.**

Above: **These Bf 109s are easily recognisable as being from 1./J88. Indeed its 2nd Staffelkapitän, Hptm. Jürgen Harder, adopted the white cross in the national insignia on the fuselage. Aircraft '6-51' ('6' being the type code for the Bf 109 and '51' its number in the unit) is being flown by Harder's successor, Oblt. Wolfgang Schellmann. Five or six victory bars are visible on the rudder, dating the photograph in mid-1938. Schellmann will eventually claim 12 victories in Spain, becoming one of the top German scorers.**

Above: **This Hs 123A, photographed on 18 February 1939, is one of those given to the Nationalist Air Force. The Hs 123 dive bomber and ground support aircraft arrived early in Spain: the first two in October 1936. Most were flown by Nationalists against Republican ground troops. Fourteen of them remained in the new Spanish Air Force after the war, and the last one served until 1952. The Spanish pilots loved the aircraft and nicknamed it 'Angelito'.**
(J-P van Mol)

CHAPTER THREE

Before the War, 1938–1939

In 1933, I had the opportunity to fly with gliders, which pleased me a lot. The next year, I joined a private aviation club, soon included in the Luftsportverband (LSV), created at that period to become the basis for the new (and still secret) Luftwaffe. In this club, I was quickly promoted to flying powered aircraft. Still as civilians, we flew the Klemm 25. This aircraft was so light and slow that we were not authorized to start if the weather was too windy! In the autumn of 1935, I had to do my military service and naturally chose the Luftwaffe [Note: this force became an official part of the Wehrmacht in February 1935]. I was in different schools and became a fighter pilot in 1937. In the beginning of 1938, as a Gefreiter, I was in 1./JG 334 whose Staffelkapitän was Werner Mölders, later to become one of the most outstanding personalities of the German fighter force [Note: I./JG 334 would become the basis for the future JG 53 Pik-As]. I was asked to become an officer but this kind of career did not attract me so much: in the Luftwaffe, I enjoyed above all things the fact that I could fly very cheaply. I chose then to become a reserve officer and had thus to stay several more months in the Luftwaffe. In October 1938, as a Leutnant der Reserve, I left the military to start my studies (technical engineering) at Aachen. I did not know that peace-time would be so shortened that I would only be able to spend one year at University. Indeed, in summer 1939, I was recalled to the Luftwaffe and posted to the German Bight area, in Oblt. von Loijewski's 5./JG 77. As a pilot in that Staffel, I would live through the first important battles against the RAF, on 18 December 1939. That day, I claimed my first victory.

(Lt. Winfried Schmidt)

Above: **Jesau, summer 1938. At this time the Luftwaffe is growing at a phenomenal rate and its units are being continuously reorganised. A typical example is I./JG 131, which will exist for only one year. In November 1938, it will be redesignated I./JG 130 before changing to I./JG 1, and in the future becoming III./JG 27.**

Gruppenkommandeur Hptm. Bernhard Woldenga is shown here in his Bf 109D, which is fitted on the left wing with a stills gun camera (the ESK 2000a Schiesskamera). Under the cockpit is the Gruppe's insignia (the Jesau Cross) which will continue to be sported by the unit's Bf 109s in the coming years.

Above: **This He 111 of KG 157 was photographed during one of the numerous exercises (*Kriegspiele*) in the pre-war period. The fuselage marking has been overpainted to show which 'side' this machine is flying for. In addition to training, the flying units also took part in special preparatory 'manoeuvres' during the tension at the time of the *Anschluss* (reunification with Austria) and the occupation of Czechoslovakia. Early He 111 models such as this would be replaced before the outbreak of World War II.**

Above: Hans Hahn joined the infantry in 1934, but like a lot of his comrades, was attached to the resurgent Luftwaffe in 1935. Transferred to the fighter force he quickly became one of the influential figures in the *Jagdwaffe* during the first three years of the war. During his career he became a popular and effective leader of a number of units (4./JG 2, III./JG 2 and II./JG 54) as well as an ace (108 victories out of which 68 were in the west). Shot down on 21 February 1943, he remained in Soviet captivity until 1949. This Bf 109E *Emil* was one of his first mounts. Photographed in 1939 it carries a chevron, indicating it belongs to a headquarters sub-unit (probably to the Stab of JG 3), as well as his personal badge on the engine cowling: a rooster.

Above: Photographed on manoeuvres in May 1939, this Bf 109 of II./JG 77 is well camouflaged at a dispersed site. Notice the thin fuselage cross and the WNr. painted on the nose tarpaulin (a luxury of the pre-war period).

Right: A Bf 109E of 3./JG 2 in the early summer of 1939. JG 2 is the Luftwaffe's fighter unit with the oldest origins, being a direct descendant of the *Reklamestaffel*. Baptised JG 2 *Richthofen*, the unit is based at this time at Berlin/Döberitz, and is tasked with defending the capital of the Reich. As such it plays no part in the campaign in Poland. Note the red 'R' in the white shield under the cockpit: all the unit's machines wear this in honour of the World War I ace.

Above: **This He 59D 'S4 + VL' was photographed at Bug am Hugen a few months before the beginning of World War II. It belongs to 3./Kb.Fl.Gr 506. In September 1939 all the seaplane units in Northern Germany will be activated to protect convoys, drop mines and attack enemy shipping. The He 59 proved to be unsuited for these roles and after a few months 3./506 will replace its aircraft with He 115s.**
(Hannibal Gude)

Above: **Built in series from the end of 1936, the Junkers 86D-1 was one of the best bomber/transport planes of its time. Nevertheless, during the Spanish Civil War it proved to be extremely vulnerable, even against biplane fighters. Despite this, the aircraft equipped a number of the Luftwaffe's bomb wings (Kampfgeschwader) in the years 1937–39 and took part in the manoeuvres preceding the Polish Campaign, as in the case of this Ju 86D-1 apparently photographed in 1938.**

Above: **I./JG 21 was created on 15 July 1939 from elements of I./JG 1 installed in Jesau. The new Gruppe soon moved to Oppeln (Prussia) where these two photos were taken. Notice the Swastika marking overlapping the rudder and fin of these Bf 109Cs or Ds, a characteristic of this period. The unit participated in the Polish Campaign and was renamed III./JG 54 in 1940.**

CHAPTER FOUR

The Polish Campaign

In July 1939, my unit, newly created I./JG
21, was based at Gutenfeld in East Prussia, to
protect Königsberg from bombing. On 1
September 1939 the war against Poland
started. At 14.36hr, our Gruppe (around 30
aircraft) transferred to Rostken, our operational airfield. At 16.16hr., we took off for
our first combat flight. We had to escort a
bomber group to its target in the vicinity of
Varsovia. When we met the bombers, they did
not identify us as friends and they opened fire.
Their gunners were very nervous on their first
(or second) war mission. Our Kommandeur,
Hptm. Martin Mettig, wanted to shoot a signal
cartridge for recognition but unfortunately it
fired in the cockpit and he was burned on his
hands, feet and thighs. He jettisoned his
canopy (with the fixed antenna mast) to evacuate the smoke but could not inform us of his
intentions. He turned and flew towards our
airfield. Half of our pilots followed him, without knowing what happened. I was amongst
them. We landed without problems.

In the meantime, the other half were involved
in an aerial dogfight with Polish PZL 24s. Four
of them were claimed shot down, but six of our
pilots had to make emergency landings and were
captured. The other pilots lost their way as the
visibility was poor; they made emergency landings, but this time behind our lines. A sad result
for our first war mission!
    (Lt. Heinz Lange, I./JG 21)

Right: **In the Polish Campaign, 5.(H)/13 was one of the
last recce units equipped with obsolete He 45s and 46s
alongside one or two Fi 156s (mainly used for liaison
flights). This picture shows He 45C '4E + CN' before a
mission over Poland. In September 1939, the unit will
lose two planes shot down by Polish ground fire. After
the campaign, the Staffel will be re-equipped with Hs
126s and the Heinkels given to flying schools. In 1942,
surviving He 45s and 46s will be included in a
Störstaffel operating by night over the Eastern Front.
These two types are thus rare examples of aircraft which
saw front-line service, were relegated to second-line
units, then later returned to a second career as front-line
machines.**
(J-L. Roba)

Above: **On 1 September 1939, the Wehrmacht invaded Poland. Among the fighter Gruppen that supported the attack
were I./JG 76 (future II./JG 54) and I./JG 21 (future III./JG 54). Both Gruppen still flew Bf 109Ds. Behind his *Dora* Lt.
Günter Scholz is preparing to make his first combat mission from an East Prussian airfield.**

Left: **This Bf 110C, presumably belonging to ZG 1, has made a belly-landing on an airfield in Poland. The propeller blades are twisted, and the wings severely damaged, but the cockpit seems to have survived the impact, protecting the crew. In the background are a Do 17 and a Fi 156 *Storch*.**

Right and below: **KG 4 fought in the Polish Campaign under 2. Fliegerdivision, stationed in Silesia. This 4th Staffel's He 111H '5J + FM' was photographed on an airfield at Oels, II Gruppe's base. Notice the markings of this period, with the thin fuselage cross. The Swastika is painted only on the fin, and doesn't overlap onto the rudder.**
(via Peter Taghon)

Above: Close to the end of the Polish campaign, three German soldiers are standing guard over a Do 17E of KG 77. This unit was created in March 1939 and operated around 100 aircraft during the Polish Campaign. It received a later model Dornier (Do 17Z) after the victory in Poland, and was eventually re-equipped with the Ju 88 just before the Battle of Britain.

Right: Fighter Gruppe I./LG 2 was often designed as I(J)./LG 2 ('J' for light aircraft or fighter). During the Polish Campaign, it was under the command of Hptm. Hanns Trübenbach, who was also the leader of Germany's aerobatic team. In September 1939, the Gruppe was based on the Malzkow (Stolp) and Lottin airfields, and their Bf 109Es quickly transferred to Polish airfields to be closer to the front line. The *Emils* shown here were photographed at Pultusk a few days before their return to Germany on 20 September 1939.

Above: Danzig, 19 September 1939. On this day, Hitler triumphantly enters the city and the Polish Campaign can be considered to have ended. II./ZG 1 participated in the campaign with its Bf 109E-1s (shown here is the mount of the Gruppenadjutant, Oblt. Erwin Bacsila). Two days later, the unit was renamed Jagdgruppe 101. In spring 1940 it reequipped with Bf 110s and was designated II./ZG 1.

Above: Aufklärungsgruppe 10 operated in the Western Campaign in May and June 1940. As with other Gruppen it was divided in three Staffeln. But, while the first two Staffeln were equipped with normal recce aircraft, 3.(F)/10 was a long-range Staffel equipped with Do 17s. Here, the Staffelkapitän passes his men in review behind a line of Do 17Ps, where one can read the code of Aufkl.Gr.10: 'T1'. Notice that the two officers wear armbands with the honour name of the Gruppe: *Tannenberg*. *(J-L. Roba)*

19

CHAPTER FIVE

The Phoney War

The plane I manned was a He 111 with the following crew: Lt. Franz Wickartz (observer and captain), Uffz. Wolfgang Just (W/Op/Air Gunner), Uffz. Helmuth Klein (Engineer/Air Gunner) and Uffz. Karl Weber (myself), the pilot. We were members of the General Wever squadron based partly at Quakenbrück. We were given the mission of observing and photographing airfields in Northern France. We took off at 09.50hr and, after avoiding the Low Countries, we entered France between Calais and Dunkirk. Weather was bad but we tried to execute the mission. After 45 minutes, the captain gave me the order to go back to Dunkirk. A few moments later, the W/Op cried that we were under attack by four enemy planes... The captain ordered me to dive but I could no longer control the plane. I turned my head to tell the Leutnant: he had been hit, and had blood in his mouth... One engine stopped and the plane flew uncontrollably. At around 2 or 3000 metres, hoping that my officer was still alive, I strapped his parachute on and tried to drop him outside. But I could not succeed in doing that. I then jumped myself and saw two attackers, a Spitfire and a Curtiss . . . I landed normally, only being wounded in the hand.

[Report made by Uffz. Weber to the Belgian authorities on 22 November 1939. His plane, He 111 '5J + FA' of Stab/KG 4, crashed at 12.20hr local time at Thorout-Kruiskens on Belgian soil. Weber was interned. The victory was attributed to two Curtiss H-75 pilots of the French GC I/4.]
(Uffz. Karl Weber)

Right: In September 1939, Oberstleutnant Carl Schumacher (a midshipman in the German Navy in WW I) is given the task of reorganising the fighter units protecting the German Bight. Situated at Jever, his headquarters commands several fighter and Zerstörer units. They will gain an important victory on 18 December 1939 during the interception of the first large RAF raid on Germany. This Bf 109E-1 or E-3 has the emblem of JG 1 (an eagle supervising the Bight and the Eastern Frisian Islands), as well as a chevron indicating the machine belongs to the Stab (headquarters).

Above: This He 111H of I./KG 53 was photographed at Ansbach at the end of 1939, having been formed from I./KG 355, which was already at Ansbach. I./KG 53 took part in the Polish Campaign, and the whole Geschwader was sent to the West in May 1940. The Heinkel in the picture has the transitional markings seen in 1939/40. The fuselage codes stand out, while the fuselage cross is still thin and the Swastika is partly on the fin.
(Karl Helber)

Right: **This Bf 109E of 4./JG 77 carries the insignias of the unit. At the front is the Gruppe emblem of II./JG 77, which is the *Seeadler* (sea eagle), and is represented by a stylised eagle's head overflying the sea. Under the cockpit is the Staffeln badge, the figure of death with his scythe, chasing the umbrella associated with British Prime Minister Neville Chamberlain. Under the camouflage paint one can see the faint outline of the letters 'O' and 'K', from the *Stammkennzeichen* – the factory code given when the aircraft was delivered.**

Left: **Leaving for a nocturnal mission on England, the Staffelkapitän and pilot of this He 111H gives the departure signal. One of the most important British targets for the Luftwaffe at the time of the Phoney War was the famous Royal Navy base at Scapa Flow. Indeed, while Germany had an effective army and air force, its naval forces were totally inferior to those of the British.**

Right: **After a short intervention in the Polish campaign, I./JG 1 was called back to Germany (to Vörden near Osnabrück) in order to protect the frontiers. Combat with French or British aircraft was rare, and the greatest problem the Gruppe had to face was the weather, which could considerably limit the operations of its Bf 109Es. Just before the start of the Battle of Britain, this unit was renamed III./JG 27, and would gain great fame under this designation.**

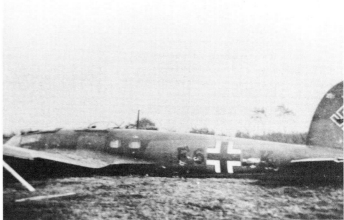

Above: While the Western front ostensibly remained 'quiet', German bombers were often engaged against British ships in the open sea or in harbour. On 9 October 1939, for instance, British cruisers and destroyers were spotted by Do I8s. No less than 127 bombers (from KG 26, KG 30 and LG 1) took off to attack them, although only a handful found the target. Around five bombers were lost, including two He 111s of II./KG 26 forced to land in neutral Denmark by lack of fuel (the crews being interned). The photo shows one of those two machines. Notice the thin fuselage cross, the position of the wing cross and the dark camouflage-colour partly hiding the fuselage codes. *(Graphopresse)*

Above: On 2 November 1939, several Hurricanes of 87 Squadron RAF took off from Lille-Seclin in order to intercept German aircraft. He 111H-2 'F6 + EK' (WNr. 5650) of 2./(F)/122 based at Münster was shot down by F/Lt. Voase-Jeff. The pilot, Oblt. Wilhelm Ohmsen, managed to belly-land near Stables. One crewman died but three others were captured. The aircraft was later dismantled by the French.

Notice the crudely painted fuselage codes. At that time, surprised by the declaration of war by Britain and France, the Luftwaffe was constantly reorganising. Many units were being disbanded or included in other existing groups. Aircraft were hastily transferred from one unit to another while hundreds of new ones were being absorbed into service. At this time, very strange codes were seen (e.g. the Bf 108 which landed near the Belgian town of Maasmechelen on 10 January 1940 and was coded 'D-NF + AW'. The Heinkel shown here ('F6 + EK') appears to have been only recently received by 2.(F)/122 and has been hastily coded before being put to use as quickly as possible. *(J-L. Roba)*

Above: In the winter of 1939–40, aircraft left in the open suffered heavily from the weather. Shown here are two Bf 110s of 2./ZG 76 at Jever in the German Bight. *(Leo Schumacher)*

Above: The winter of 1939–40 was particularly rigorous. The climate limited aerial operations while aircraft and men suffered in the cold. The Luftwaffe used this quiet time to reorganise its units and equip them with more modern equipment. This He 111 of KG 27 at Lechfeld is protected from the snow, and is also camouflaged to escape the attention of regular Allied reconnaissance flights.

Right: If, at the beginning of the war, many German aircraft had been quickly painted, this was not the case for this neat – and rare! – Do 17S-O reconnaissance aircraft. 'T5 + FH' of 1.(F)ObdL had started a mission to England on 13 January 1940 but was shot down by Curtiss H-75s of the French Groupe de Chasse I/4. The pilot, Lt. Theodor Rosarius, made a good landing near Calais and was captured with his crew. Only three Do 17S-Os were built.

As with many other German POWs in French hands, Rosarius was liberated at the end of July 1940 and returned to flying duties. He gained his fame later in the war when he became the CO of KG 200, the special unit equipped with captured enemy aircraft (the notorious *Zirkus Rosarius*).
(Presse Francaise)

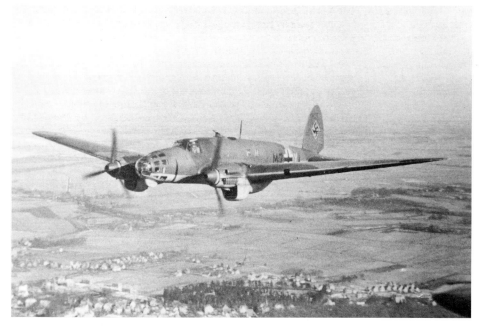

Left: By the beginning of 1940, all He 111 bomber units had been re-equipped with the later 'H' model. Older models (such as the 'B' shown here) were in the main relegated to training or second line units, although some served in operational units as transport and liaison machines. This He 111 seen flying over Northern Germany wears the code 'M7 + YL', indicating that it belongs to 3./K.Fl.Gr.806, a maritime unit equipped at that time with He 60s, He 114s and He 111s. The Staffel soon converted completely to He 111s before becoming 9./KG 54 in September 1942.
(Hannibal Gude)

Right: Mechanics are working on this Do 17Z which was damaged after the port undercarriage collapsed. The fuselage codes '5K+CP' indicate that it belongs to 6./KG 3. Note the highly visible bright yellow letter 'C', the identity mark of the 6th Staffel.
(J-L. Roba)

23

Above and below: **On 25 April 1940, Lt. Erich Pristaat of 4.(F)/121 got lost during a recce mission over France. Believing that he was above Germany, he landed his Do 17P '7A+ BM' at Tintigny in Belgian Luxembourg. The country being neutral, the crew was interned while their aircraft was examined by the local authorities, who were especially impressed by the three superb precision cameras. Note the sharp-edged camouflage paint, the white outline to the black 'B' code, and the serial number painted on the nose. On 10 May 1940, the first day of the invasion of Belgium by the Wehrmacht, the local guards blew up their prize.**

CHAPTER SIX

The Campaign in the West

On 15 May 1940, I took off at 14.35hr to attack an armoured column near Gembloux (Belgium). I was attacked from the front by Spitfires who had eight guns firing at the same time. My propeller stopped turning and I landed diagonally in a meadow surrounded by hedges. The area was under fire by German artillery. With my gunner Liebberenz, we left the aircraft, bringing our MG gun with us. Liebberenz went back to the Stuka to get more ammunition while I placed the weapon in position. For the first time we heard the combat noise that our unit could make. It was terrific. Suddenly, I saw one Ju 87 landing close to us. I sent my gunner to the spot. He ran to the Stuka and climbed into the plane which started immediately. In order to gain some height, they had to overfly the enemy position and in doing this, the aircraft was hit many times. (I would hear later that it had to land as soon as it reached German lines.)

In case of a possible emergency landing on an enemy position, I had brought in my Ju 87 a 1kg bomb with which to destroy the plane if necessary. I was preparing the charge when I heard above me a fearful noise. I saw a Ju 87 falling vertically in flames. The tanks in the wings blew up in a big explosion. I would later learn that the pilot of that Ju 87 was my Staffelkapitän, Oblt. Merz, killed in this action. A Stuka split off from the formation and landed close to me. I thought at first that the aircraft had been hit and obliged to land, but it was not the case: the pilot wanted to pick me up. I ran to the machine to climb in, near the gunner's seat. We also started overflying the enemy position and were hit several times. I was sitting on two metal helmets and was hardly shaken when they were hit by bullets. In spite of the several hits, we reached our airbase. I thanked my rescuers and said: 'Who knows, it is possible that I could one day repay you in the same manner'.

(Valerian Dill, SG 2 Immelmann)

Right: **On 9 May 1940, the paratroopers of 9./FJR 1 wait patiently on Gütersloh-Rehda airfield. They will soon be loaded onto the Ju 52s of KGzbV 1, from which they will drop on targets in the Netherlands. The campaign in the West is due to start on the following day – 10 May 1940.**

Above: **In the early hours of 10 May 1940, the Luftwaffe attacks. Waves of bombers take off to destroy Allied and neutral airfields in France, Belgium and the Netherlands. Even though surprise is achieved, the Luftwaffe loses many aircraft. But it has gained the advantage, and its casualties will diminish in the coming days. Here a He 111 is photographed from the nose gunner position on another.**

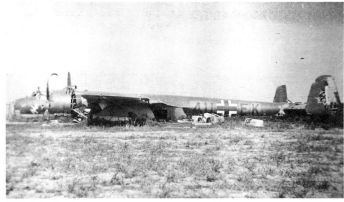

Above: In the first days of the campaign in the west, the German High Command needed as much information as possible on the position and movements of enemy troops. All the Luftwaffe's reconnaissance units were heavily utilised, and many aircraft were lost. 2. (F)/123 was based in München-Gladbach in and flew missions in VIII Fl.Korps. In 37 sorties (13 on the first two days of the attack), it lost three planes. Two crews were killed, but the men who flew Do 17P '4U + FK' had more luck. Attacked by French Morane MS-406s on 12 May 1940, Fw. Bournot managed to belly-land his damaged plane at Mettet near Namur (Belgium). He and his two crewmen were captured by French troops. But as with many other German soldiers who fell into French hands, they were liberated the following month. Bournot's crew returned to duty and continued to fly in the Mediterranean. His unit, one of the first to be formed in Hitler's Luftwaffe, was officially disbanded on 13 January 1945.

Notice the insignia on the nose of Bournot's wrecked Dornier (an eagle holding a telescope on a two-coloured shield). Near it is painted a white number (perhaps the serial). Note also that the fuselage codes are freshly painted, perhaps over those of another unit.

(Yves Empain)

*Above: **Operation Niwi** was an unconventional action launched by the Wehrmacht on 10 May 1940. A special unit of Fi 156 Storch liaison aircraft was assembled, along with a detachment of the Grossdeutschland Regiment. Two soldiers were loaded in each tiny machine and, in the first hours of the Westfeldzug (the invasion in the West), the fleet of around 100 Störche were sent to land in the Ardennes behind the Belgian lines. Niwi was not very successful, mainly because the lead pilot lost his course and half the machines landed in the wrong place. The others were able to shuttle in some 260 men of the Grossdeutschland but the attacking forces were dispersed. They nevertheless managed to cut communications lines and seize key points, all of which disrupted communications and liaison between Belgian and French troops. A few Fi 156s crashed or were shot down by ground fire, and one of them is seen here at the side of a road filled with a column of Belgian refugees. On the original image the white number '16' is just visible on the tail fin. These codes were painted on to help the infantrymen find their own particular aircraft.*

Below: Among the 24 Gruppen equipped with He 111s which took part in the campaign in the West, KG 1 *Hindenburg* operated over Belgium and Northern France. Subordinated to I. Fl.K. (HQ at Cologne), the unit suffered heavy losses in the first days of the attack. At least eight aircraft (including that of the Commander of the IIIrd Gruppe) were downed on 10 May 1940.

Above: During the *Westfeldzug*, older models (eg. He 45s and 46s) of reconnaissance and liaison aircraft attached to infantry units were withdrawn from front-line use. They were replaced by Hs 126s and Fi 156s. Shown here is a Fi 156 *Storch* of 1. (H)/Aufklärungsgruppe 41, attached to IV. Armeekorps during the attack on Belgium. 'C2 + PH' has just landed near the headquarters of the 8th Infantry Division to make an urgent report.

Below: A family portrait. On an improvised airfield in May 1940, the crew of a Flak gun asked the pilot of this Bf 109E (belonging to II./JG 53 *Pik-As* 'Ace of Spades') to take their photograph. After putting his parachute on the tailplane, he captured the scene. Note the rear-view mirror above the cockpit canopy.
(J-L. Roba)

Above, left and right: **This Bf 110 'A2 + IH', belonging to 4./ZG 52, was forced to belly-land after suffering combat damage. The landscape indicates that the aircraft came down in the Belgian or French Ardennes. On 16 May, the Luftwaffe shifted a large number of units toward the Sedan sector, which became the *Schwerpunkt* ('heavy point') of the attack. Heavy fighting took place, resulting in the loss of many French, British and German aircraft around this border town.**

Above: **A French soldier inspects a Ju 88 shot down (presumably by GC I/2) at Auberive in May 1940. The insignia shows that the bomber belonged to KG 51, the *Edelweiss* Geschwader. This unit was part of V. Fliegerkorps and was based in Bavaria at the beginning of the Western Campaign. KG 51 had its IInd Gruppe completely equipped with Ju 88s, the IIIrd having only He 111s and the Ist a mix of both types.**
(Gaston Botquin)

Above: On 21 May 1940, the Bf 109E of Major Erich Mix (Gruppenkommandeur of III./JG 2) was severely damaged during a dogfight above the French countryside. Injured, Mix (who had flown as a fighter pilot during World War I) succeeded in belly-landing his aircraft . Visible on the wrecked machine is the Geschwader insignia, an 'R' under the cockpit for *Richthofen* (the honour name of JG 2). The double chevron indicates that the aircraft belongs to the Gruppenkommandeur, while to the rear of the *Balkenkreuz*, the wavy line identifies a III Gruppe machine.

Above: May 1940. A Bf 109E of 2./JG 76 has made a perfect belly-landing in a field in Northern France. The pilot presumably escaped unhurt. Under the cockpit of 'Red 7' is the Gruppe's crest. On 10 May 1940, I./JG 76 was based at Ober Olm and the CO was Obstlt. Kraut. In mid-1940, the unit was incorporated in JG 54, becoming II Gruppe of that Geschwader. The insignia remained with it.

Above: Having suffered battle damage in the heavy fighting, this Ju 87B of I./StG 77 is being repaired on an improvised airfield at Egem in Belgium. On 9 May 1940, I./StG 77 was based with the rest of the Geschwader at Cologne-Butzweilerhof, but quickly moved to advanced airfields to harass the retreating Allied columns.

Left: Continually flying over enemy front lines in order to observe troop movements, the *Heeresaufklärung* units suffered many casualties. This Hs 126 was forced down in a field (maybe in Western Belgium), although it appears that the crew survived the crash landing.

Right: Chosen by Adolf Hitler as his personal pilot, Hptm Hans Baur commanded the small unit of transports (FW 200, Ju 52, etc) attached to the Führer's staff. Here, FW 200 Condor '26 + 00', one of the best-known of Hitler's planes, has landed on the airfield at Regniowiez (in fact a large meadow). Situated in France, but very near the French-Belgian border, this was used for liaison and transport aircraft in June 1940. Indeed, at that time, the Führer's HQ was situated in the nearby Belgian village of Brûly-de-Pesches (codename: *Wolfsschlucht*). Notice the two-bladed propellers on the Condor.
(J-L. Roba).

Left: After the end of the Western Campaign, there was much damaged war material which could be recovered. A German soldier photographed this Ju 87 as it was brought back toward a dump near Dunkirk. In order to facilitate its movement by road, the Stuka has had its wings taken off.

Above: **Here Bf 109E 'Yellow 5' of an unknown 3rd Staffel (identifiable by the colour of the number and the lack of horizontal bar after the *Balkenkreuz*) is also recovered. It is being towed by truck through a French town, and it too has had its wings 'amputated'. Note that the retractable undercarriage legs have been tied together for the journey.**

Above: **In July 1940, after the victory in the West, German soldiers inspect a Do 17 of 9./KG 76 which made a belly-landing in northern France. The recovery teams of the Luftwaffe will have a lot of work to deal with all the wrecks lying in Belgium, the Netherlands, Luxemburg and France. Surprisingly, a handful of these machines will remain *in situ* until the end of the war, never having been recovered by the Germans. *(via Rèmy Chuinard)***

Below: **Symbolising the German victory in the West, a Heinkel 111 Staffel of KG 55 *Greif* overflies Paris.**

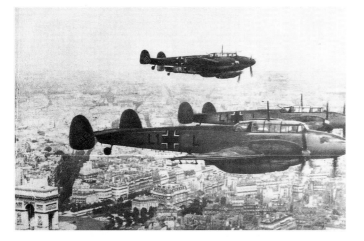

Above: **A *Schwarm* of Bf 110s of 3./LG 1 'parades' above the Arc de Triomphe in Paris. Note that the wartime censor has attempted to erase the 'C' next to the *Balkenkreuz* on the aircraft at the foreground. Unfortunately, they must have known little about Luftwaffe markings: this letter was the least informative of the four. Here 'L1' indicates the Geschwader (LG 1) and the 'L' the 3rd Staffel.**

Above: **After the Fall of France, 7./LG 2 began to re-equip with the Bf 110. This crashed aircraft 'L2 + NR' shows the unit's insignia (the devil's head) on its mottled camouflage. It also has a white nose.**
(J-L. Roba)

Above: When the Germans captured Bourges, they found the French assembly line for the Curtiss H-75 fighter. Shown here is a H 75A-4 repainted in German markings. Within a few months, the Luftwaffe tried to equip some front-line units with the American design. In mid-1940, II./Tr.Gr.186 became III./JG 77 and received around 30 of the Curtiss machine. But the trial was not successful, and the aircraft was disliked by the German pilots. After a few incidents, they were retired and III./JG 77 again received Bf 109Es.

A handful of Curtisses were used as French fighters in the German propaganda film *Kampfgeschwader Lützow* (made by Karl Ritter), while others went to German flying schools, remaining in use till around 1943. In 1941, some were sold to Finland.
(via Gaston Botquin)

CHAPTER SEVEN

The Battle of Britain

On 18 July 1940, I started from Dinard at 0.30hr in the third aircraft. The weather was poor again. We flew towards the Channel. We met the first clouds at 300m. We climbed at 2.5m/sec and crossed four or five cloud strata. The earth was no longer visible. After 1.35hrs flying time, we reached a height of 5000 metres. At about 2hrs we sighted the English coast. Through holes in the clouds, I could see several spotlights. Now the cloud cover became less. After ten minutes, I saw facing me and slightly to the right several red Morse signals. One of these gave the letters 'MA'. I had already thought that our course was too much to starboard. I looked on the map, starboard of our planned course, for a place with its name beginning with 'MA' lying in the area we were overflying. I found the name 'Shepton Mallet' around 30km to the right of our planned course, south of Bristol. Carefully, I changed direction 20 degrees to port. Immediately the Bristol Channel came in sight, as the sky was by now cloudless.

Set course to Swansea. Over our target, we found again a layer of clouds which was certainly not big, especially in the face of the Anti-Aircraft- searchlights. In spite of the balloon barrage, we decided to dive. The lowest clouds were at 2,000 metres. I could identify without any doubt Swansea Bay. We went over our objective and I dropped my bombs at 2.25hr: 2 x SC 250 and 10 x SC 50. In the target area, we could observe one large fire. We now had to fly for five minutes in the face of the defensive searchlights. The AA fire became heavier and some shots exploded close to us. We flew seawards and then in the direction of St Malo. Soon after, we were out of the lights and we again gained some altitude, until we reached about 4500 metres. We overflew Jersey Island at 3.25 hr and landed at 4.40hr, some minutes after sighting the signal 'AV' for Avord. We were the third plane to land, and the only one to have dropped bombs. We heard also that the Geschwaderkommodore had fallen in the Bach (Channel). We slept from 6.00hr to 14.30hr and were again on duty at 18.30hr.
(Fw. Heinrich Rödder, 8./KG 27)

Above: This Ju 87B 'A5 + KK' of 2./St.G. 1 was probably photographed in August 1940 on the French airfield at Dinard (Brittany). I./St.G. 1 had a very active life. Raised in 1939 at Insterburg, it took part in the Polish Campaign before being sent to Luftflotte 3. Fighting in the Norwegian campaign under Luftflotte 5, I./St.G. 1 was at Trondheim when the *Blitzkrieg* was launched in the West.

In summer 1940, the complete Geschwader was assembled from various subordinate units. I./St.G. 1 was called to the West to operate from Angers under Luftflotte 3 with Stab and III./St. G.1 (II./St.G. 1 was at that time part of Luftflotte 2 in the Pas-de-Calais). St.G. 1 suffered heavy losses over England, which gave rise to the idea that the Ju 87 was obsolete and outclassed. British fighter opposition and the problems of a long flight over the English Channel had posed insuperable problems to the dive bombers. But the *Stuka* remained a front-line machine, deadly as long as the Luftwaffe had some degree of air superiority. In the winter of 1941–42, I./St.G. 1 was renamed II./St.G. 3 and operated successfully in North Africa. *Stukas* wreaked havoc over the USSR, and also sank many Royal Navy vessels in the eastern Mediterranean. On the Western Front, they fought right up to the end of the war, although in the latter months they could only survive by flying at night. Notice that the aircraft in the photo is fitted with long-range fuel tanks under the wings.
(J-L. Roba)

Above: A Heinkel 111H of KG 27 flying towards England. Dispersed between Tours, Dinard, Bourges and Rennes, this Kampfgeschwader was under the command of Oberst Behrendt.

Above: **These bomber crewmen, wearing their flying suits, are waiting for the orders to scramble on a mission against England. When taking the picture, the photographer has tried to avoid identifying the unit, leaving the Ju 88s way in the background. But, on the far left a wooden panel has been painted with the *Edelweiss* insignia of KG 51. The photograph must have been taken on one of Orly, Melun-Villaroche or Etampes-Mondésin, the three airfields around Paris occupied by the Geschwader.**
KG 51 was heavily engaged over England, losing 51 planes (destroyed or at least 50 per cent damaged) in four months of fighting. On 29 March 1941, the whole Geschwader moved to the East to take part in the Balkan operations.
(PK)

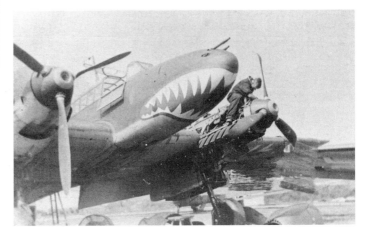

Above and right: **As was common at the beginning of the Battle of Britain, these Bf 110s of II./ZG 76 have a shark's mouth insignia painted under the nose. This Gruppe flew against England from the French bases at Caen and Abbeville, as well as from Guernsey. Called back to northern Germany during the next winter, the unit fought over Crete, while its 6th Staffel was detached to fight the British in Iraq.**

Right: This Bf 110, 'L1 + AK' of 14.(Z)/LG 1, is having its guns tested and aligned on the airfield. V.(Z)/LG 1 suffered heavy losses during the Battle of Britain before being disbanded in October 1940, shortly after its Kommandeur's (Hptm. Horst Liensberger) death. The unit's survivors were called back to Germany in order to build the nucleus of the nightfighter Gruppe I./NJG 3.

Left: Not all Bf 110s were given to the *Zerstörer* units, some went to recce squadrons to replace their Do 17s. An example is this aircraft of 7./LG 2. Equipped with Dornier 17s until July 1940, the unit moved to two airfields near Brussels (Evere and Grimbergen) to train on the Bf 110 before flying missions over England. Note the Staffel emblem on the nose: a devil's head having its origins in the Spanish Civil War.

Right: In the summer of 1940, a red band around the engine cowlings of the Bf 109Es of III./JG 53 covered the *Pik-As* emblem. Operating in the main from Guernsey, the Gruppe claimed around 270 victories from July to December 1940. Nevertheless, its casualties were heavy, with nearly 50 pilots killed, missing and injured, plus another 30 shot down in England and captured. The pilot of this aircraft was more lucky: he just made it back to the French coast before running out of fuel. At least he avoided ditching in the *Bach* (Channel), always a risky affair. The short range of the Bf 109 made running out of fuel an ever-present hazard, and forced landings such as this were a frequent occurrence.

Above: In the first stages of the Battle of Britain (July/August 1940), I./KG 40 was established on the Brest-Guipavas airfield in Brittany. But the base was too near England, while its installations were unable to cope with the heavy four-engined FW 200 *Condors*. So the unit moved to the airfield of Bordeaux-Mérignac, which became its most renowned base. From there, I./KG 40 flew intensive operations against British shipping, earning for the FW 200 the nickname 'The Scourge of the Atlantic'. From the summer of 1940 to the end of spring 1941, those bombers were credited with around 200 ships sunk. Often attacking at mast height, the FW 200 eventually lost much of its potency at the end of 1941 in the face of Allied countermeasures.

Note here the highly visible insignia of I./KG 40.

(Peter Taghon)

Above: In the heat of the summer of 1940, a Bf 109E of the Geschwaderadjutant of an unknown unit (presumed to be JG 77) takes off on a mission to Britain. The fighter's acceleration on the dry ground raises a significant dust cloud.
(PK)

Above: The Luftwaffe lost many aircraft over England, although in fact the Battle of Britain was not so damaging as the campaigns in France, the Netherlands and Belgium. The significant difference was that all aircrew that baled out or crash-landed in Britain became POWs, with no chance of escaping over German lines. A prison camp was almost certainly the fate of the crew of this Ju 88 which made a belly-landing in Kent in August 1940. Men of the Home Guard (the so-called Dad's Army!), civilians and children are happy to be photographed near the fallen giant.
(J-L. Roba)

Above: Propaganda played a powerful role with all the combatants in World War II, although many feel that the best action films were made by the German *Kriegsberichter* (war correspondents). They often flew, sailed or drove with the troops, and many were killed in action. The 'KB' shown here is about to set off on a mission to England in a Ju 87B of I./St.G. 1 (code '6G'). He is most probably working on the *Wochenschau* (the newsreel shown each week in the cinemas of Germany and the occupied countries). To give the camera a clearer view, the rear of the canopy has been removed. During the Battle of Britain, II./St.G. 1 was deployed on various airfields in the French Pas-de-Calais.
(PK)

Right: **A II./ZG 2 crew poses on a Bf 110 clearly marked with the unit's emblem. This unit was known as II./ZG 2 from June 1940, previously being identified as III./JG 334, I./JG 143, I./ZG 52, Jagdgruppe 52 and I./ZG 52 again from the beginning of 1940, when it switched from the Bf 109 to the Bf 110.**

Left: **Dornier 17Z-3 '5K + JH' (WNr. 2807) of 1./KG 3 photographed on the Belgian airfield of Le Culot (Beauvechain). KG 3 was deployed on various airfields in Belgium (Deurne, St Trond and Le Culot) for operations against England. This aircraft was sent on the first night operations over Britain, and crashed as it returned to Grand Mesnil during the night of 28 August 1940, killing its pilot and one other crew member. It was the first 'Belgian' victim of what became known as the *Blitz*.**

Right: **Having suffered many casualties by day, the Luftwaffe turned to night bombing. For this role, many aircraft were partially repainted black. This He 111 of KG 55 was apparently photographed in the vicinity of Paris (Chartres, Dreux or Villacoublay). Most of its codes have also been painted over, apart from the 'F', the individual identity letter for this aircraft. The fuselage crosses and the Swastikas were often covered too.**

Above: Probably photographed near Dinard (Brittany), this crash-landed He 111H-2 of I./KGr.100 seems to be in remarkably good condition. It is under armed guard, but the camouflage net cannot obscure the unit's crest: a *drakkar* or Viking longship. KGr.100 was the first 'pathfinder' unit in Luftwaffe service. Note the distinctive three antennae (the *Dreimaster* He 111) which formed part of the radio guidance system to lead the pathfinders to the target. This photograph was probably taken during the Battle of Britain, the plane having been damaged after a mission over England.
(J-L. Roba)

Above: On Dinard airfield (in Brittany), two groundcrew carry a container (presumably loaded with incendiary bombs) from a He 111 of II./KG 27. Notice the dark paint on the underside of the wings, engine nacelles and fuselage.

Above: The Fi 156 *Storch* was used not only as a liaison plane, but also as a flying ambulance. This white 'stork' was attached to JG 2 in France at the end of 1940. Note the civilian codes, the large red crosses and the absence of all defensive armament.
(Dr Hofner)

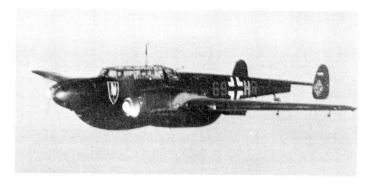

Above: At the end of 1940, the Luftwaffe needed to create a nightfighter force to counter the increasing weight of RAF attacks. The first unit raised was NJG 1, whose leader was the night-fighting pioneer Major Wolfgang Falck. Bf 110 'G9 + ER' shown here is one of the first aircraft of 7./NJG 1. It still has the *Dackelbauch* ('basset belly') extended fuel tank. Note the insignia of the nightfighter arm, the *Englandblitz* (a diving eagle holding a lightning fork).

Below: Two officers of the Kriegsmarine talk in front of Do 17P '6M + GL' of 3.(F)/Aufkl. Gr. 11. One of them wears a parachute indicating that he is about to fly as a crewman. The presence of Naval personnel in Luftwaffe recce aircraft was not uncommon where missions were directed against convoys. Usually, these were carried out by *Seeaufklaürer* (sea reconnaissance) units, although in 1940–41, they were also flown by normal recce crews. 3.(F)/11 took part in the Polish campaign (in Heeresgruppe Nord), in the Norwegian campaign and in the attack in the West (attached to 6. Armee). In the Battle of Britain, the unit was one of the three *Einschiessen der Küstenartillerie am Kanal*, specially tasked with spotting and correcting the fire from German coastal batteries in the Channel. This photo, taken in the first months in 1941 probably shows the preparation for such an operation.
(PK)

Above: During the Battle of Britain, many aircraft came down in the Channel, and the Luftwaffe (and the RAF) used seaplanes to search for and rescue downed crews. The Germans began by painting red crosses on their rescue planes, in the hope that the RAF would leave them alone. Unfortunately, the seaplanes could not resist the temptation to radio back the location of any convoys or shipping they flew over, so the RAF regarded them as legitimate targets. The red crosses were quickly abandoned, and the aircraft returned to more conventional markings, like those on this He 59 anchored in Boulogne harbour. In the winter of 1940–41, the sea rescue units were reorganized into specialized *Seenotstaffeln*.

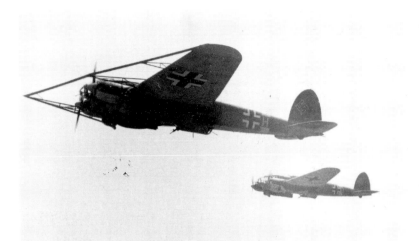

Left: In low-level attacks, German bombers often suffered losses and damage when flying through balloon barrages. So the idea was born to equip He 111s with a framework to act as a cable fender and cutter. In early 1941, all Kampfgeschwadern operating in the West received a handful of these He 111H-8s. The modification was not a success, and in fact only 30 machines were produced. The device weighed around 135lb (300kg) and had to be balanced by an equivalent weight of ballast in the tail. The extra weight and drag hampered the manoeuvrability of the bomber and limited the bomb load. A few He 111 H-8s were lost over Britain, then in mid-1941 the survivors (around 25 of them) were sent to the rear to act as glider tugs. In this propaganda picture, one H-8 is shown in its projected role, flying ahead of a formation of 'conventional' bombers. *(via Peter Taghon)*

Right and below: Although the FW 189 *Uhu* (owl) reconnaissance and liaison aircraft gained its fame in Russia, it actually began its operational career over England in the first months of 1941. These FW 189As belong to 1.(H)/Aufkl. Gr. 12 (code 'H1'), which from the end of 1940 was based at the Belgian airfield of Aalter (near Ghent). At this time 1.(H)/12 was taking the *Uhus* to replace the HS 126s it had flown in the Polish Campaign. After some operations against England, the Staffel moved to the east in May 1941 to take part in *Operation Barbarossa*. *(Karl Meyer)*

CHAPTER EIGHT

Norway, 1940–1941

On 13 September 1940, three Blackburn Skuas were reported at 17.13hr arriving in Square 50 111-06 East. At 17.15hr, a Schwarm led by Lt. Georg Schirmböck took off to protect Bergen. Over this area were several clouds and a heavy rain diminished visibility to 1km. Victim of the bad weather, Lt. Schirmböck hit the sea with his propeller blades and the damage forced him to fly back to base. He landed at 17.45hr and led the rest of the mission by radio. Uffz. Niemeyer took command of the three aircraft as he had the better radio and had a better knowledge of the area. The Kette flew further over the Bergen area and, at 18.05, it sighted two Blackburn Skuas. Uffz. Fröba and Uffz. Niemeyer were attacked by one of those. While Uffz. Fröba defended himself in a dogfight, Uffz. Niemeyer could attack. At 18.10hr, the enemy plane landed on the sea near the Western side of the Asköy Island (Quarter 5151) after having been hit by Uffz. Fröba. Both crew members were picked up in their dinghy by a German ship. Uffz. Fröba and Uffz. Niemeyer carried on with their protection mission and were finally ordered to land at base (landing time: 18.23hr).

The second enemy plane was attacked and shot down by Fw. Haarbach. It at first dodged by diving into a large cloud. But Fw. Haarbach turned around and waited until the reappearance of the enemy. After about 15 minutes, he sighted the Blackburn Skua trying to escape, diving and flying at low height. On the sixth attack, the British aircraft turned over on one wing and crashed on the ground in Square 5119 at 18.25hr. Feldwebel Haarbach landed at his base at 18.55hr.

(Staffelofficer of 4./JG 77)

Right: **He 115 of 1./K.Fl.Gr. 106 photographed in Stavanger. This Staffel operated in the torpedo strike role in *Weserübung*, acting under Küstenfliegergruppe 506. It seems that the Staffel did not remain long in Norway, returning to Germany after a few weeks. Even though it already looked obsolescent, the He 115 was produced up to 1944.**
(Verrycken via Van Mol)

Above: **In order to prevent the supply of iron ore being cut off by the Allies, Germany decided to intervene in Scandinavia. *Operation Weserübung* actually took place only 24 hours before the French and British landed their own troops in Norway! Surprise was the watchword for the German operation, with many troops being flown in by air.**

Transport units played an important role, and formations such as KGzvV 1, 101, 102, 103, 104, 105, 106 and 107 all took part. On 9 April 1940 at Neumünster airfield, JG 2 pilots photographed these soldiers boarding Ju 90s belonging to Lufthansa. These civilian aircraft formed part of KGzbV 105 (which was also in possession of the only Ju G-38 used in this role). A few days later, the Ju 90s operated alongside FW 200s to bring urgently-needed supplies to German troops at Narvik.
(Hans Assi Hahn)

Left and below: To protect the bombers and transports engaged in *Weserübung*, the Luftwaffe deployed the Bf 110s of ZG 1 and 76. The sole Bf 109 unit operating in this campaign was II./JG 77, commanded by Major Harry von Bülow-Bothkamp (a combat veteran from WW I). The photos show his personal aircraft at Christiansand. He was originally scheduled to leave the unit at the end of March 1940, but rather than replace him in the middle of the campaign, the High Command extended his tenure until mid-1940. He then went to take command of JG 2, and three weeks later, he was leading the *Richthofen* Geschwader in the heavy fighting of the Western Campaign.
(Von Bülow family)

Left: For *Operation Weserübung* (the invasion of Denmark and Norway), Fliegerkorps X (Generalleutnant Hans Geissler) commanded two Bf 110 units, I./ZG 1 and I./ZG 76. The long range of the twin-engined fighter was a valuable asset, and this example from 3./ZG 76, photographed at Stavanger-Sola, shows how it was increased further. The Bf 110 has two extra tanks under the wings as well as the huge *Dackelbauch* under the fuselage. The tanks themselves reflect the colour scheme of the aircraft, with their upper surfaces being painted in dark green.
(Meyer via Knut Maesel)

Above: **Uffz. Reinhold Schmetzer of 5./Tr.Gr. 186. II./Tr.Gr. 186 was sent to Norway in order to reinforce German forces after many units were recalled to fight in France. Schmetzer poses before the wreck of a He 111 of KG 26. Aircraft destroyed during the Scandinavian campaign were collected in a dump before being repatriated for scrap.**

Right: **In mid-1940, II./Tr.Gr.186 moved to Norway to reinforce the German fighter units based in that newly conquered country. Mechanics of the Gruppe are seen here before a Ju 88, perhaps belonging to KG 30. It is obviously a replacement machine sent to fill the gaps after *Operation Weserübung* as it still has its *Stammkennzeichen* (delivery codes) 'CH+??'. Notice the white number '043' on the nose (purpose unknown).**

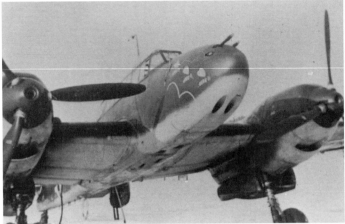

Left: **When the Luftwaffe invaded Scandinavia, three Kampfgeschwadern (4, 26 and 30) were deployed in the North. Here, Ju 88s of KG 30 are photographed somewhere in Norway. The unit (under the command of Obstlt. Loebel) was first based at Westerland. It flew extensively against shipping and in support of Dietl's ground troops, but was quickly recalled to Germany in May to fight in the Western Campaign.**

Right: **In early 1941, 1.(Z)/JG 77 (ex-*Kommando Kjevik*) is created at Christiansand in order to protect the Norwegian coast. In February 1941, the unit is sent to Mandal to be nearer to Lister and the principal RAF targets in Norway. This photo of a Bf 110 dates from around this time. It still carries the emblem worn originally by II./ZG 1 (three wasps above a cloud) which will disappear from the unit's Bf 110s in mid-1942.**

Left: **This FW 200 *Condor* 'NK + NM' was photographed on the Stavanger airfield. While its exploits as a long-range bomber are renowned, its role as a transport is less well known. The fuselage codes (and the drapes behind the fuselage windows!) indicate that this machine was used as a VIP transport.**

Right: **At the height of the fighting over Southern England and the Channel, German units based in Denmark and in Norway carried out numerous patrols to protect naval convoys and harbours from the Blenheims and Wellingtons of RAF Bomber Command. On 23 October 1940, Gefr. Heinrich Brunsmann belly-landed his Bf 109 'Black 8' at Tronheim-Vaernes. Note that the runway has a wooden covering, a typical practice on northern European airfields to counter the problems caused by snow.**

Above: Lt. Karl-Fritz Schloßstein of 1.(Z)/JG 77 is photographed at Kjevik in the cockpit of his Bf 110. Note the Revi reflector gunsight in front of his face. Schloßstein acts as leader when his Staffelkapitän, Oblt. Felix-Maria Brandis, is called to headquarters or is on leave (as was the case in November 1941).

Above: The crest of KG 26, a lion with the motto *Vestigium Leonis*, is visible on this photo of a He 111 of an unknown Gruppe. This bomber unit is often associated with the Scandinavian Campaign, and it operated as a torpedo unit against Allied convoys bringing supplies to Murmansk. Later, its Heinkel 111s and eventually Ju 88s and 188s, flew operations in the Mediterranean and in Romania.
(J-L. Roba)

Above: When the Kriegsmarine was planning the aircraft carrier *Graf von Zeppelin*, a special variant of the Bf 109 was developed to operate from its decks. The Bf 109T *Toni* had an arrester hook under the fuselage and an extended wingspan (36ft/11.08 metres as against 32ft/9.87 metres for the Bf 109E). When it became clear that the ship would not be completed, the aircraft were transferred to front-line units, especially to I./JG 77 based in Norway. This Bf 109T 'Black 5' of 2./JG 77 is shown in the autumn of 1941 on the wooden runway at Lister.

CHAPTER NINE

Marita-Merkur – The Balkan Campaign of Spring 1941

I came to 6./JG 77 at the beginning of 1941 and my first real campaign was the Operation Marita, i.e. the invasion of Yugoslavia and Greece. At the end of April, the British troops were evacuating the mainland. On 24 April, I participated in a great operation over Athens. My Emil was hit by AA fire and I had to parachute to safety. Nevertheless, I was wounded and quickly captured by some Anzacs (Australian or New Zealand soldiers). I was lying in a hospital when three Greek officers came near my bed. One of them was a medic. They told me that I had to be their prisoner because it was a Greek gun which had blown me from the air! The British personnel had no time to discuss the problem and so I was transferred to a Greek military hospital. It was my luck. When it evacuated, the Allied Expeditionary Force left with all its POWs, sending them to Egypt where they spent the rest of the war. I remained only a few days in Athens and, when the first German motorcyclists entered the Greek capital, I saluted them from the hospital balcony. So I was freed! I later came back to the Staffel just in time for the invasion of USSR. I claimed there my first victory. [He ended the war as a Major credited with 102 victories and wearing the Knight's Cross.]

(Lt. Siegfried Freytag, 6./JG 77)

Right: In order to support the attack on Greece and Yugoslavia (*Operation Marita*), all the flying units were assembled in Luftflotte 4 (General der Flieger Alexander Löhr). To reinforce the bomber forces (mainly KG 2 and KG 51), I./LG 1 was deployed from the west to operate under VIII Fliegerkorps. This 'experimental' unit was based in Bulgaria at Plovdiv-Krumowo. On 28 March 1941, Uffz. Heinz Abracht made a bad landing after a training flight and crashed his Ju 88A-4 on the airfield. Notice the Geschwader insignia (the coat of arms of Pomerania, ie. a red griffon on a white background) and the number '38' painted on the nose.
(Gerd Noschinsky)

Above: Seven Ju 87 Gruppen took part in the Balkan Campaign. They proved their effectiveness in the mountainous terrain by making pin-point attacks against strongholds and military columns trapped on steep-sided roads. Here a *Stuka* Staffel of St.G.2 is overflying Mount Olympus.

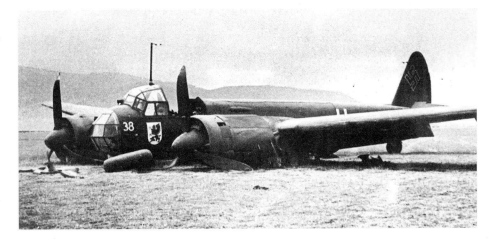

Above: When *Marita* began, the German High Command faced severe logistic problems. Balkan roads were usually primitive, while the sole railroad going through Yugoslavia to Athens was often attacked and cut. The only reliable way to bring in supplies was by air, and every available transport unit was put to use. These Ju 52s of IV./KGzbV 1, coded '1Z + BF' and '1Z + B (A?)' are seen on a Greek airfield being loaded with barrels of fuel. Visible on the nose of '1Z + BF' is the unit insignia, a devil on a bomb. Notice the light grey paint and light-coloured rudder on this aircraft. *(PK)*

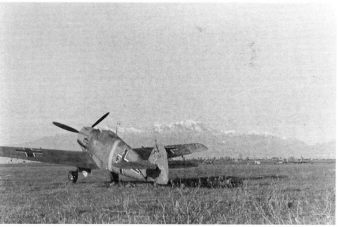

Above: Although it belongs to III./JG 77, this Bf 109E *Emil* photographed on Skolpje runway in mid-April 1941 bears under the cockpit the 'R' emblem of JG 2 *Richthofen*. The horizontal bar after the *Balkenkreuz* (the normal marking of the IInd Gruppe) will soon be replaced by a wavy line (the usual marking of the IIIrd Gruppe). Note the yellow-painted engine cowling, rudder and fuselage band.

Left: From 16 to 21 April 1941, III./JG 27 was based at Kozani airfield, where this photo was taken. In the background is Bf 109E-4/B (WNr. 785) of the Gruppenstab. Its engine cowling (presumably white) bears a chevron and a vertical bar, the usual markings of the Geschwaderadjutant.

Above: Fi 156 *Störchen* proved to be very useful in the *Marita* campaign. These early STOL aircraft could land on tiny patches of flat ground, such as on the quays of Aegean harbours. While the crew of 'KD + SH' waits for orders, another machine is taxiing for takeoff. The place may be Volos harbour in Greece.

Below: The Balkan and Cretan campaigns will see the intensive use of paratroopers. Coming from the sky with little or no warning, they will often surprise the Greek and Commonwealth defenders. Shown here is the drop to capture the bridge over the Corinth channel. Even though the attackers managed to take the bridge, the defenders were able to destroy it first.

Above: On 27 April 1941, in a lull between the Balkan Campaign and the attack on Crete, pilots of III./JG 77 travelled to Vienna to take charge of newly delivered aircraft. One of them took this photograph of He 70 'BV+GO', belonging to an unknown unit. *(ISKEN)*

Above: After the British were chased from the Greek mainland to the island of Crete, there was a pause while Hitler considered his next move. An assault on Crete would be costly, tying down forces and supplies needed for the planned invasion of Russia. But the decision was taken, and the attack went ahead, codenamed *Operation Merkur* (Mercury). This picture shows the airfield at Molaoi in the Peloponnese, a typical front-line base of the time. The Bf 109Es belong to III./JG 77, although the one in the foreground was transferred from JG 2 (and still wears the 'R' badge), and the one behind comes from a *Schlacht* unit (see the triangle). During this time, on 10 May 1941, Rudolf Hess (Hitler's Deputy) flew to Scotland in a Bf 110 to try and negotiate a separate peace.

Left and above: In order to support the massive drop of *Fallschirmjäger* in Crete, several Ju 52s towed combat gliders. The main glider was the DFS 230, which had performed successfully in the capture of the forts on the Belgian border (May 1940). Warned by the decoding of German *Ultra* messages, the British defenders had concentrated their strength on the dropping zones, and it may be that the gliders saved the operation for the Germans. Hostile fire was not the only hazard, however, as Generalleutnant Süssmann, the CO of FJR 3, was killed on 20 May 1941, at the beginning of the operation, when a tow cable snapped. These photos of gliders DFS 230s after the battle show their simple, lightweight, and cheap construction. Note the almost complete absence of national markings, just a small cross on the fuselage.

49

Left: After the paratroopers were dropped on Crete, they desperately needed reinforcing. *Gebirgsjäger* (mountain troops) were sent by boats to the south of the island. After the Royal Navy destroyed one flotilla, the *Gebirgsjäger* were flown to Maleme airfield by Ju 52s. Here, mountain soldiers are pulling on their life-jackets before boarding a Ju 52.

Right: This view of Maleme airfield shows the slaughter suffered by the German transport units. British defenders brought down large numbers of these aircraft, while others were destroyed when they collided with the wreckage strewn across the airfield. The consignment of mountain troops may have saved the paratroops, but the whole Cretan operation cost 271 transports (some 10 Gruppen worth). These machines would be sorely missed during the upcoming invasion of the USSR.

Left: At the end of *Marita*, Stab and II./JG 27 were called back to Germany, and played no part in *Operation Merkur*, the invasion of Crete. III./JG 27 flew to Gela (Sicily) to operate for around 20 days over Malta (the Gruppe fought alongside Müncheberg's 7./JG 26). One of the most active pilots of III./JG 27 was the Staffelkapitän of 9./JG 27, Oblt. Erbo Graf von Kageneck, seen here in front of his Bf 109E-7 (WNr. 4187). Notice the yellow nose and the victory bars on the fin. Erbo was the daredevil of his family and joined the Luftwaffe in 1936. He started the war in 2./JG 1 (later 8./JG 27). He distinguished himself in France (4 kills), in the Battle of Britain (9 kills) and over Malta (4 kills). He fought in the Russian Campaign, where he received the *Ritterkreuz* and added the Oak's Leaves three months later. On Christmas Eve 1941 he was wounded in a fight with a Hurricane over Agedabia (Libya). Transferred to Naples, he died on 12 January 1942 in an Italian hospital, after developing blood poisoning from his wounds. Initially buried in Naples, he rests today in the Caira war cemetery (near Monte Cassino).
(August Graf von Kageneck)

CHAPTER TEN

The Invasion of the USSR, 1941–1942

After my training at Königsberg, Brieg and Weimar-Nohra, I joined 1.(H)/12 as an air gunner. At that time (February 1941), the Staffel was on the Belgian airfield of Aalter (near Ghent) and equipped with FW 189 Uhus (all the Hs 126s of the preceding year had disappeared). I had good relationships with my two other crewmen, Gefr. Ellerich (the pilot) and Fw. Lotter (the observer). We mainly flew missions alongside the Dutch/Belgian/French coasts. In May 1941, the complete unit moved to the East at Graudenz without knowing that the invasion of the USSR would start soon. We received maps and were ordered to study with great attention the geography of the area. On 23 June 1941, the 2nd day of Operation Barbarossa, the sun was shining when we started in the early hours. We flew for around 30 minutes when our FW 189 was hit by AA guns. The pilot tried to fly as long as possible in the hope of reaching our lines. We were afraid to fall into enemy hands: we had already heard several rumours of lynchings of shot-down German pilots. [Author's note: Indeed, several experienced Luftwaffe pilots were shot in their first hours of captivity during the first days of Barbarossa; among others, Major Wolfgang Schellmann, Kommodore of JG 27 and Ritterkreuzträger]. We finally had to land but in enemy-held territory. We quickly left the plane and moved off to the west. We were lucky and avoided all Soviet patrols until we rejoined our lines! We then moved to Kowno and launched many missions – around three a day – for Heeresgruppe Nord. The most dangerous operations were in the early morning. Indeed, we had to fly eastwards facing the rising sun. We could not see our adversaries and soon the Soviet pilots learned that weakness. They then waited for us in the morning, always attacking from the sun where we were blinded. We suffered many losses and, in November 1941, were called back to the West, this time to a French airfield near Paris. We were based there for around six months before flying back to the Eastern Front in summer 1942. On 12 July 1943 I received the Deutsche Kreuz im Gold and my comrade Lotter was later awarded the Knight's Cross.

(Ofw. Karl Meyer, 1.(H)/12)

Above: When Operation *Barbarossa* (22 June 1941) began, the single-engined fighter force had been partly re-equipped with new aircraft. If JG 27 (Luftflotte 2) and JG 77 (Luftflotte 4) still had the Bf 109E *Emil*, JG 3 (L.Fl. 4), JG 51 (L.Fl. 2) and JG 54 (L.Fl. 1) had the new 'F' (*Friedrich*) version. This *Friedrich* of 7./JG 54 is seen during the early phases of *Barbarossa*. Notice the green heart insignia of the Geschwader and the crest of III./JG 54 (what was I./JG 21). *(Hans Biederbick)*

Above: Seen from the rear gunner seat of another, a Ju 87B of St.G. 2 flies in close formation returning from dropping its bomb.

Above: During the war, the meteorological reconnaissance units (the *Wekusta* or *Westa*) used a range of different aircraft (including He 111s, Do 17s and Ju 88s). For *Barbarossa*, Luftflotte 4 had *Westa* 76 with six He 111s, five Ju 88s and three Bf 110s (based at Reichshof). One of these Ju 88s, '5Z + MA' crashed in June 1941 and was severely damaged. Notice that the individual aircraft identifying letter is painted on the yellow fuselage band, which is positioned much further forward than normal. *(Brunsmann)*

Above and right: In July 1941, while landing at Jassy airfield, this Bf 109F of 8./JG 77 nosed over. Luckily, its port wing went deep into the soil, preventing the aircraft tipping right over onto its back and possibly severely injuring the pilot. Note the yellow-painted wing tips.

Right: **Oblt. Wolfdieter Huy (StK. of 7./JG 77)** is seen on 5 July 1941 during the ceremony of his award of the Knight's Cross. His Bf 109F (WNr. 8334) bears nine victory bars, as well as silhouettes of ships damaged or sunk during the earlier campaigns in the Aegean. This aircraft will be transferred in 1942 to 4./JG 77 and will be completely destroyed on 7 June of that year.

Left: To honour the German fighter pilots based on their soil, King Mihai (Michael) of Romania and his Prime Minister, General Ion Antonescu, visited I./LG 2 and III./JG 77 at Jassy. Major Alexander von Winterfeldt welcomes the visitors. In the background is a Ju 87 of the St.G.77, which was based on the same airfield.

Right: As they advanced into the heart of the USSR, German forces discovered how simple and efficient much Soviet weaponry was. A good example was the Il-2 *Sturmovik*, a tough ground attack aircraft which proved to be resistant to ground fire and fighter attack. The one shown here was captured in the southern sector of the front, and is an early single-seat variant. Along with a few others, it was repainted in German markings and studied carefully, mainly at the Rechlin test centre. Later Il-2s had a rear gunner, which at first surprised German fighter pilots who attacked them from behind. A number became victims of this defensive fire, including the great ace of JG 54, Oblt. Wolfgang Spaete, who had to belly-land after such an encounter.

Left and below left: **1.(H)/12 fought in the northern sector of the Eastern Front in support of XXVIII. Army Corps. The FW 189s of the Staffel carried the unit's crest, a Turk playing a flute, which was devised in honour of the Staffelkapitän, Hptm. Ruff, who knew the Turkish language.**
(Karl Meyer)

Below right: **A Ju 87 *Stuka* squadron overflies the improvised Ukrainian airfield of II./JG 3 at the beginning of *Barbarossa*. Included in V. Fliegerkorps (along with KG 51, KG 54 and 4. (F)/121), JG 3 fought in the southern sector.**

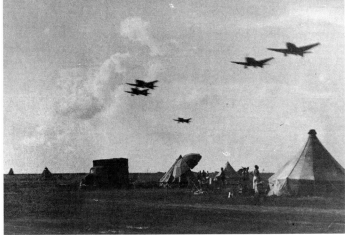

Above: **On 12 July 1941, Oblt. Heinrich Sannemann (Stk. of 6./JG 3) attacks a Soviet bomber in his Bf 109F-2 'Yellow 1'. During the attack his armoured windscreen is hit by defensive fire. Despite the loss of visibility, Sannemann succeeded in landing his aircraft safely at the airfield at Miropol. It is quite clear from this picture that the armoured glass probably saved his life.**

Below: **At the beginning of the war, many believed that the neutrality of the Red Cross would be respected by the belligerents. Aircraft used as flying ambulances or in air-sea rescue roles were often painted white, with civilian markings and large red crosses. But cruel reality soon made its presence felt, and the flying ambulances had to be remilitarised and camouflaged, although they often kept their red crosses. A typical example is this Fi 156 photographed somewhere in the USSR (notice the yellow fuselage band).**
(J-L. Roba)

Left: **Coming back from an operation in June 1941, the port engine of this Ju 88 of KG 51 caught fire. Ground crew on the airfield at Zilistea (Romania) used foam extinguishers to fight the fire and rescue the aircraft. KG 51 originally came from 5. Fl.K. in Poland, but was later transferred to 4. Fl.K. operating from Romania.**

Right: **SS infantrymen examine the wreckage of this Bf 109F, bearing the chevron and vertical bar of a Geschwaderadjutant. The *Pik-As* badge on the cowling identifies the aircraft as belonging to JG 53. This may be the crash of 15 July 1941 when Oblt. Wilfried Pufahl (Geschwaderadjutant of JG 53) had to make an emergency landing after combat over Tyranowka.**

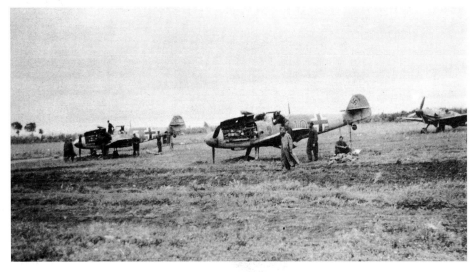

Left: **Bf 109Fs of I./JG 52 are propped up at the *Justierstand* (weapons adjustment stand). JG 52 was one of the youngest squadrons of the fighter force, although it eventually became one of the highest scoring, with around 10,800 victories through the war. Note how the fighters have their main wheels dug into the earth to prevent the recoil from their guns pushing them backwards.**

Right: **As well as the combat machines, the Luftwaffe had hundreds of aircraft on the Eastern Front which carried out more peaceful tasks. This Bf 108 *Taifun* was probably used for liaison or postal (*Kurriermaschine*) duties. 'RC + YZ' (WNr. 2110) has belly-landed somewhere in Bulgaria or the Ukraine and seems to have survived the landing relatively intact. Note the personal insignia (a man's head looking over the moon). (Brunsmann)**

Left and below: **Gen. Oberst Alexander Löhr's Luftflotte 4 comprised two aerial corps. One was IV Fliegerkorps of Generalleutnant Kurt Pflugbeil, with two fighter units, namely JG 77 and I./LG 2, as well as a bomber unit: KG 27 (including II./KG 4). This corps was based in Romania and reinforced by the Romanian air force. The initial advance into Bessarabia and the Ukraine was very quick, and units were rapidly displaced eastwards. These He 111s belong to KG 27 *Boelcke* and are operating from Poltava in the Ukraine. They are carrying the yellow fuselage band adopted in April 1941 on all Luftwaffe aircraft used over the Eastern Front.**

Left: Waffen-SS soldiers examine the wreck of a Ju 88A-4 of KG 77. Above the crest is a ribbon with the unit motto 'Ich will dass si vorfechten'. On the eve of *Barbarossa*, KG 77 was included in I. Fliegerkorps (HQ Gumbinnen) alongside KG 1, KG 54 and KG 76. *(Pierre Tiquet)*

Right and below: For *Barbarossa*, the Stab and the three Gruppen of KG 76 were part of I Fliegerkorps based in East Prussia. At that time the Geschwader was equipped with Ju 88s (the year before, it flew with Do 17Zs). These aircraft of 6./KG 76 were photographed at Orscha, probably around October 1941. At that time the unit had been shifted from attacking Leningrad to support the ground troops advancing toward Moscow. But by now the weather had turned, and many airfields had to be lined with logs to prevent the aircraft being stuck in the thick mud.
(Hellmuth Müller via P. Taghon).

Above: On the eve of *Barbarossa*, Stab, II. and III./KG 1 were in East Prussia under I. Fliegerkorps, although until June 1941, the unit had flown over Britain. This Ju 88 is seen in September or October 1941, when KG 1 *Hindenburg* operated in the area around Leningrad. The unit will carry out bombing attacks around here for many months.
(via J-P. Van Mol)

Below: The numerous markings and decorations on this Bf 109F of JG 54 should please any modeller. On the engine cowling it wears the 'winged shoe' of the 7th Staffel, while under the cockpit is the badge of III Gruppe (three aircraft on a cross). It also has the yellow fuselage band and behind the cross, the 'streamer' of a IIIrd Gruppe. Note that the spinner and cockpit hood have been removed, leaving the barrel of the engine-mounted cannon protruding at the front.

Above: Even as most of the Luftwaffe's combat strength was committed to the offensive, I./LG 2 wa sent to Mizil and Mamaia on 30 July 1941 to defend Rumanian territory against Soviet attacks. This Bf 109 *Emil* of 2./LG 2 was photographed at Mizil airfield. It carries the characteristic mottle camouflage that the Gruppe wore until mid-1943 (even after it became I./JG 77 in January 1942). Behind the fuselage cross is the squadron's 'top hat' badge which originates from the Spanish Civil War. Under the cockpit is the Gruppe's emblem: an 'L' over a silhouette of Britain, which recalls the unit's operations against England until mid-1941.

Below: The huge distances and poor road network of the Soviet Union caused the Germans great problems in keeping their units resupplied. And as summer turned to autumn, rain and mud made the problems worse. As well as transport planes, the Luftwaffe made use of gliders, such as this DFS 230 on the grass runway at Sarabus (Ukraine). As on most German gliders, the identification markings are only a small fuselage cross and a narrow yellow band. Note the (unidentifiable) badge under the cockpit.

Right: Groundcrew Hubert Ernsting is photographed by the heavily decorated rudder of this Bf 109. The fighter is flown by Oblt. Kurt 'Kuddel' Ubben, Stk. of 8./JG 77. During the early months of *Barbarossa*, this unit scored many victories for few losses, Ubben scoring the 40th (against an I-153) on 2 October 1941 at 11.56hr. As the rudder indicates, he has already been awarded the *Ritterkreuz*, which he received on 4 September 1941.

Left: This Fi 156 is fitted with an auxiliary fuel tank and bears a large yellow fuselage band with the cross on it. The badge on the nose seems to be that of JG 51, which implies that this aircraft may have been a 'hack' of the *Mölders* Geschwader.

Right: On 15 July 1941, Obstlt. Werner Mölders became the first fighter pilot to achieve 100 air-to-air victories. Three weeks later he was appointed Inspector of Fighters and forbidden to make any more combat flights. Despite this ban, he continued to fight, winning several more victories which were not officially claimed. Here he is shown arriving at Sarabus airfield, in a borrowed JG 3 fighter, to meet with III./JG 77's officers. On 22 November 1941, Mölders took off from Sarabus in a transport He 111 to take part in the funeral ceremony of General Ernst Udet. Caught in a storm, the twin-engined aircraft crashed at Breslau-Gandau, killing the crew and their famous passenger.

Above: **This FW 44 *Stieglitz* is parked in the orchard of a Soviet village, and probably used the main street to take off and land. Normally used in the training role, this one is the 'hack' transport of 7./LG 2. Coded 'L2 + XR', it has a yellow fuselage band and has its individual identity letter in white. It also carries the unit's 'devil's head' emblem.**

Above: **By October 1941, the first signs of winter are appearing at the improvised airfield at Sechtschinskaje (125 miles/200km to the west of Orel). The cold increases wear on the engines, so the mechanics of II./JG 3 run them for some time to warm them up before take off. The Bf 109F in the foreground has a yellow spinner, while that on the aircraft behind appears darker. Note the unusual camouflage on the engine cowling, and the Gruppe's emblem (derived from the family emblem of the first Kommandeur, Major Erich von Selle).**

Above: **On 2 November 1941, the Bf 109F of Lt. Wolfgang Kretschmer (Erg. Staffel JG 54) was hit by AA fire above Neva in the Leningrad area. Despite the damage, the pilot was able to belly-land on the snow-covered airfield at Siverskaja. The E-Staffel was disbanded on 9 March 1942, its personnel and equipment dispersed to the three Gruppen of the Geschwader. The E-Staffel achieved a total of 51 victories.**

Above: **Winter and bad weather caused special problems for seaplanes. If surprised by the cold, flying boats or float planes could be trapped by the ice and were sometimes damaged or even destroyed. This He 115 of a *Seenotstaffel* avoided such a fate and is shown sitting on the ice at Reval, waiting for a mission.**
(Gerhard Huth)

Right: **After the heavy losses the Transportgeschwadern suffered in Crete, they were faced with worse problems on the Eastern Front. In late 1941, large numbers of German troops were surrounded and cut off in the pocket around Demjansk. On 16 and 17 December, flying schools were combed to raise new transport units in order to supply the men in the 'pocket'. The new units were known as KGzbV 600, 700, 800, 900 and 999. This Ju 52 of KGzbV 900 ('X8 + GH') is operating in typical winter conditions, having landed on a frozen runway. During the resupply operation, 262 transport aircraft were lost. Two Gruppenkommandeure were killed, while 383 crewmen became casualties. Nevertheless the aerial bridge was regarded as a success, although it was to create a false sense of optimism when German armies were besieged later in the war, especially at Stalingrad and in Northern Africa. On these occasions, air supply was not enough to avoid disaster.**
(J-L. Roba)

Left: During the terrible winter of 1941–42, a Henschel Hs 126 of 4. (H)/23 warms its engine before taking off from an improvised runway in the Demjansk pocket. Note the winter camouflage (which covers the yellow fuselage band) as well as the lack of undercarriage spats, which were usually removed in winter to prevent snow and ice jamming the wheels. At that time 4. (H)/23 belonged to NAGr. 8, and later became 2./NAGr. 5 in September 1943.

Right: Ofw. Johann Pichler (7./JG 77) prepares to board this Bf 108 of III./JG 77, as he departs for some well-earned leave. At this point (winter 1941–42) Pichler has around 20 victories. This quiet, older pilot, who started the war as a truck driver, was awarded the *Ritterkreuz* on 19 August 1944. He ended the war with 52 victories (of which 25 were scored in the West).

Left: A Bf 109F of 8./JG 52 after a belly-landing in the USSR. III./JG 52 was involved in the Cretan Campaign, and remained in Romania until July. The unit then joined the Russian invasion in the lower-Dniepr and Poltava, where it scored many victories.
(via Pierre Tiquet)

Right and below: In the first quarter of 1942, 9./KG 51 operated in the southern sector of the Eastern Front, attacking shipping along the Crimean coast. In March of that year, the unit was supported by the transfer of Hptm. Werner Baumbach of KG 30, a specialist in this type of operation. Ju 88A-4 '9K+AS' warms its engines on a Ukrainian airfield (perhaps Nikolajew). Notice the KG 51 *Edelweiss* crest and the open entry hatch, which is also the lower rear gunner's position.
(Hans Höger)

Right: When the Hs 129 ground-attack aircraft was first developed, it proved to be severely underpowered. Its salvation was the capture of large numbers of Gnome-Rhone engines after the fall of France. The Hs 129B, with French engines, was produced in 1941. In the Soviet campaign, 5. and 6./Schlachtgeschwader 1 (raised in January 1942) were equipped with the Hs 129B-1. Shown here is Hs 129B-1 'Blue C(?)' (WNr. 0191) of 5./Sch.G. 1 after a belly-landing on 23 May 1942 near Konstantinowka. The twin-engined 'tankbuster' had been hit by Soviet AA. Notice the insignia (a bear with an axe) and the fuselage triangle, worn by many *Schlachtflieger* machines.
(J-L. Roba)

Left: As the war dragged on, many front-line soldiers and airmen couldn't get leave to go home and marry their sweethearts. One solution was the proxy wedding, where the serviceman would be married with his commanding officer officiating, while at the same time another ceremony took place in Germany with the girl present. The proxy wedding shown here is taking place in a *Schlacht* unit. The new husband stands between his two witnesses in front of a Hs 129, which has the *Schlacht* badge on the nose.
(Albert Palm)

Right: Photographed in the USSR during 1942, this Henschel Hs 123A-1 'Yellow K' belongs to 7./Sch.G. 1. Unlike the 5th and 6th *Staffeln*, this unit was still equipped with these obsolescent biplanes. The *Staffel* was led by *Ritterkreuzträger* Lt. Josef Menapace; it operated in the central sector of the Eastern Front, and from July 1942 in support of the drive on Stalingrad. In mid-October 1943, II./Sch.G. 1 was renamed II./SG 2. Note the ground attack badge on the fuselage.

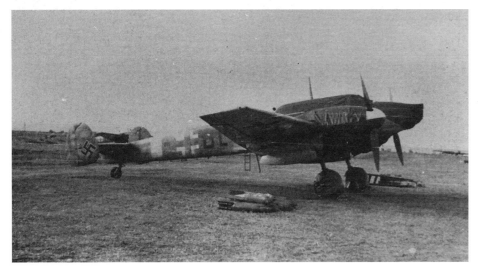

Left: A Bf 110 sits protected by tarpaulins on an exposed Crimean airfield. The tiny codes '6M + BL' indicate that this twin-engined aircraft belongs to *Küstenstaffel Krim*, a reconnaissance unit created locally to operate along the Crimean coast. The presence of bombs may indicate that the Staffel flew attack missions as well as reconnaissance flights.
(Dan Antoniu)

Above: Do 17P-1 coded '1R + AH' in spring 1942 belonging to the Aufkl. Kette (F) *Lappland* (a recce unit based at Lapony in Finland). In January 1943, this unit became part of 1.(F)/Aufkl.Gr. 124.

Above: Mid-1942, and a Bf 109F of II./JG 77 at Kastornoje is manhandled by mechanics on a very primitive runway. At this time, most of the aircraft still bore II Gruppe's badge, the *Seeadler*, which dated from the 'Phoney War' when the unit defended the Baltic and the North Sea.

Above: Near Voronezh, in the summer of 1942. A Staffel of Aufkl. Gr. (H)/32 celebrates the unit's 1000th combat mission flight. Notice the height of the Hs 126 and the ladder needed to climb into the cockpit.
(J-L. Roba)

Above: Heinz Klöpper is a relatively unknown Luftwaffe ace, although he gained 79 victories in his short career. Posted to 2./JG 77 at the beginning 1940, he was severely injured in the French Campaign. He rejoined his unit at the end of the Battle of Britain, where he won his first officially confirmed victory. When I./JG 77 was renamed IV/JG 51 (note the little cross after the *Balkenkreuz* on his aircraft, indicating a IVth Gruppe), he gained fame on the Russian Front from the summer of 1942. Notably, he claimed 5 victories on 7 July and a further 25 in August. Here he poses near his rudder, adorned with 62 victory bars (the last one having been gained against an Il-2 on 24 August 1942). He was awarded the *Ritterkreuz* on 4 September 1942, having gained his 67th *Abschuss*. Send to the Western Front, he gained another 12 victories before being killed on 29 November 1943 while acting as Staffelkapitän of 7./JG 1.

Left: Krasnogwardeisk, in the autumn of 1942. This Bf 109F 'White 9' of 1./JG 54 carries the green heart (the Geschwader's emblem) as well as I. Gruppe's badge. Smiling in his aircraft, Uffz. Karl Schnörrer was one of those quiet and devoted pilots who permitted the top aces to make the most of their abilities. A long-time wingman of Walter Nowotny, 'Quax' Schnörrer ignored many opportunities to score, to ensure the security of his leader. Nevertheless, he achieved 46 victories and eventually received the *Ritterkreuz* (22 March 1945).

Right: **At the end of the summer of 1942, III./JG 77 received improved fighters, namely Bf 109G-2s. Some were fitted with MG 151 20mm cannon in underwing gondolas. Two aviators of 7./JG 77 (Fw. Heinz Furth and Ofw. Johann Pichler) pose in front of such a newly arrived *Kanonenboot* (cannon ship). It already wears the Gruppe's emblem: a wolf's head, based on the family emblem of the former Kommandeur, Alexander von Winterfeldt.**

Above: **Winter 1942–43. Fw. Reinhold Höger is strapped in before taking off in his Bf 109G of I./JG 54. His aircraft is temporarily camouflaged with washable white paint which covers the insignia on the cowling. During his time on the Eastern Front, Höger took part in many combat operations, claiming one or two victories. After this, he was sent as an instructor to an *Ergänzungsjagdgruppe*, EJG Ost, a training unit based in Southern France. On 28 October 1943, the 24-year old pilot was killed when he crashed into the sea off Biarritz.**
(Hans Höger)

CHAPTER ELEVEN

The Mediterranean, 1941–1942

The Jabo-Gruppe OBS (Fighter Bomber Group of High Command South) was placed directly under the orders of Generalfeldmarschall Albert Kesselring. I joined the unit in October 1942. On the Comiso (Sicily) airfield was also a Gruppe of JG 53 Pik-As. The mission of the Jabo-Gruppe was principally to attack the airfields of Malta to destroy the airpower on the island. As the attacks led by 'normal' bombers (for instance He 111s) were very costly, we had to do the same task with our agile Messerschmitt Bf 109s. I flew my first war flight on 25 October 1942. As with every other day, it was hot and no clouds hung in the sky. My 1st Wart (mechanic) helped me equip myself (signal pistol, ammunitions, survival rations, etc.). I began to sweat heavily. I entered the plane. My mechanic was sitting on the wing waiting for the order of my Schwarmführer (leader of a formation of four planes). After a few minutes, he raised the hand, shut the canopy and jumped off the wing. I started then. Under my Bf 109F-4 'N 12', a 250 kg bomb. We took off at 16.25hr and, after a turn to the left, assembled over Sicily at 3000 metres. Then we headed south in a continually climbing course to gain 7000 metres. In the cabin, the temperature was warm. When we were still over Sicily we could see in the far distance the island of Malta. We were escorted by some fighters of JG 53. We liked their presence because with the bomb under the belly, our planes were not very manoeuvrable. When we were near Malta at 7000 meters, we heard on the W/T 'Achtung, Indianer über Gozo' ('Attention, Indians over Gozo'. Indians was the code name for enemy fighters). We knew that they could attack coming from the sun. Our Schwarmführer found the assigned target: Luqa airfield and we began to dive from around 6000 meters at the speed of 700 kph. Our ears were whistling. We met an AA barrage of all types of guns. At around 1500 meters, we dropped our bomb; then we pulled the stick with both hands to fly north to the sea and come back very low over the waves to Sicily. British fighters appeared for the attack. They had waited for us over the northern coast of Malta and dived from above to shoot us down. I could see the impact of the

bullets around me in the sea. But we had no time to begin a dogfight as we had not enough fuel. I saw the Sicilian coast coming nearer and nearer. By that time, the British fighters had already left. I landed at 17.17hr. The nervous feeling ended. I went then to the Debriefing. Following the escort fighters, we had placed some hits on the airfield. We had suffered no loss in this operation.
(Uffz. Werner Zirus, pilot in Jabo-Gruppe OBS)

Above: **At the beginning of February 1941, 7./JG 26 is sent to the Mediterranean to reinforce the German units supporting the Italian Air Force. It was first based at Gela (where this photo was taken), then in Italy, then in Greece at the end of May. After this it crossed the Mediterranean to Libya, where it fought for two months. Scoring 52 victories without a single loss, the 'red heart' Staffel (note the emblem on the engine cowling) achieved resounding success.**

Below: **When General Erwin Rommel took command of his expeditionary corps in Northern Africa (the future Afrika Korps), 2.(H)/14 was his sole Luftwaffe recce unit. The Staffel flew both short and long range missions with a mixture of aircraft (Hs 126, Fi 156, Bf 110). Shown here is Fi 156 *Storch* '5F + YK' of the recce unit overturned after a bad landing or after a sudden desert storm. The engine and landing gear have already been dismantled, and the airframe has been written off as a total loss.**

Right: A large part of 7./JG 26's successes on the Mediterranean Front was due to Oblt. Joachim Müncheberg, Kapitän of the Staffel and one of the greatest aces of the Luftwaffe. He is photographed at Gela during the spring of 1941 after a victorious mission over Malta. From 12 February to 6 May 1941, he claimed 19 victories above the island.

Left: The greatest problem facing Axis troops in the African campaign was the reinforcement and supply of the motorised units engaged in the advance to Egypt. Convoys *en route* to Africa had to be protected from British airpower based at Malta. Here a Bf 110 of ZG 26 is seen flying over such a supply convoy. To increase its range, it is equipped with two additional tanks under the wings. ZG 26 was often deployed between Africa and Sicily (or Crete) to cover a large area of the Mediterranean.
(PK)

Right: After Crete fell into German hands and after the ground advance along the African coast, the Luftwaffe could operate from both sides of the Libyan Sea. Aircraft could set off from Libya, attack any shipping they found, then land in Crete. They could refuel and rearm there before making the return trip, along with a second attack. Raids were so intense that the Royal Navy nicknamed that part of the Mediterranean bomb alley. Here Bf 110s of ZG 26 are assembling on a Libyan airfield before such a shuttle operation.
(J-L. Roba)

Left: One of the most useful aircraft in Rommel's inventory was without doubt the Ju 87 *Stuka*. It was able to make pin-point attacks against Allied positions and on supply columns on the narrow coastal roads (such as the *Via Balbia*). His Ju 87s and their crews were extremely successful, and several pilots were awarded the *Ritterkreuz*. Here a Ju 87 of an unknown unit (St.G. 1, 2 or 3) is seen flying over Libyan waters. *(J-L. Roba)*

Right: Malta was the Achilles' heel of the Wehrmacht in the Central Mediterranean. But the demands of the Eastern Front soaked up most of the Luftwaffe's strength, and the forces deployed against Malta suffered. The individual units deployed changed constantly, and joint German-Italian missions often had to be carried out. Here a Ju 87 of II./St.G.1 is escorted by an Italian Fiat G-50 of 358 Squadriglia. *(PK)*

Left: The sturdy three-engined Ju 52 was one of the most ubiquitous aircraft in the Western desert. Not only did it bring troop reinforcements to the front line, but it also carried fuel and all sorts of war material. Aircraft returning to Europe were often loaded with wounded. This *Tante Ju* wears the crest of IV./KG zbV 1. Notice the rear mirror used when towing gliders.

Above left: **In the African desert, the Luftwaffe had to adopt new camouflage schemes. As the Italian Air Force had flown in the region for many years, the Germans often copied Italian schemes, such as the well-known 'sand and spinach'. This FW 58 *Weihe* is an interesting example of such an attempt.**
(PK)

Above right: **The distances covered in the desert campaigns were huge, and units were often lost or separated from the main forces. The tiny Fi 156 *Storch* was intensively used by the Germans to locate units, carry orders and messages, transport officers (including such senior figures as Rommel or Kesselring), and even rescue downed aircrew. Allied forces also valued the tiny STOL aircraft, repainting and putting into use any that they captured intact. This picture shows Fi 156 'NO + OL' of a liaison unit under guard for the night, while the crew and others have a brief rest on the desert sand.**
(PK)

Right: **The rudder of Lt. Friedrich Körner's Bf 109F photographed at Martuba during the spring of 1942. Körner belonged to I./JG 27 along with the famous ace Hans-Joachim Marseille, and was able to develop his own fighting skills to a high pitch. He claimed 36 victories over African soil before he was shot down and captured on 4 July 1942, two months before he was due to be awarded the *Ritterkreuz*. Note the silhouette of a tank above the normal kills, the four bars indicating the number of such fighting vehicles destroyed.**

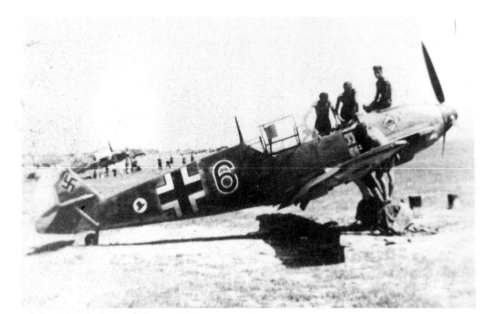

Left: **The markings on the front of this Bf 109E indicate that it belongs to JG 53; but towards the tail is the 'hat' insignia of 2./JG 77. Indeed, I./JG 77 left the Eastern Front in July 1942 to operate over Sicily. From there, its Bf 109Fs flew over Malta gaining some victories but also suffering losses. This yellow-nosed *Emil* was perhaps an old machine of the *Pik As* given to the incoming Gruppe. (Walter Fuss)**

Above: **Bf 109F 'Black 11' of Lt. Friedrich Körner (2./JG 27) being refuelled.**

Right: **After Adolf Galland, Hans-Joachim Marseille was probably the best-known Luftwaffe ace. This colourful character joined the Luftwaffe in 1938 but ran into disciplinary problems until he was sent to Africa. Here he was given enough freedom to show his remarkable abilities as a fighting airman. He downed 158 allied aircraft overall (of which 151 were in Africa) before being killed. On 30 September 1942, while flying back to his airfield, his Bf 109G's engine caught fire and Marseille baled out. He hit his head on the tail of the fighter, and was killed when he fell unconscious to the ground.**

Above and below: **Uffz. Hans Hempfling, born in 1916, came very late to the fighter arm.
He joined 3./JG 77 at the end of August 1942, and operated over Malta. He is seen here on
a Sicilian airfield with two Bf 109G-2s. From 1941, the Gruppe adopted its distinctive
camouflage: green patches over sand, which lasted on some aircraft until 1944.
Hempfling followed I./JG 77 to North Africa in October 1942. He claimed around three
victories there, but was killed in action on 14 January 1943. Notice the insignia of I./JG 77
which was the crest of the ex-I./LG 2 ('L' for Lehrgeschwader over the outline of Britain).**

Left: **The Bf 109F (WNr. 8573) of the legendary ace Hans-Joachim Marseille in September 1942, with 136 victories on the rudder.**

Right: Scramble at Martuba in the spring of 1942. Pilots and mechanics of I./JG 27 rush toward their Bf 109Fs lined up close to the sandy runway.

Below: In the quiet waters of Elmas harbour (Sardinia), a Do 24 of 6. Seenotstaffel waits for its next operation. The pilot's and gunners' positions are protected from the heat by tarpaulins. 6. Seenotstaffel flew in the Western Mediterranean and picked up downed aircrew from all air forces as well as survivors from sunken ships. *(Alessandro Ragatzu)*

Above: The impressive Blohm und Voss 222 *Wiking* flying boat was produced in very limited numbers, and was used for the transport of men and supplies. They were mainly flown by Lufttransportstaffel See 222 (created in June 1942), but the big six-engined machine proved to be easy prey for Allied fighters. The one shown here is moored in Tobruk harbour. Note the B&V (Blohm & Voss) symbol and the *drakkar* (Viking) insignia.
(J-L. Roba)

Right: It is often stated that Italian aircraft that served in the Luftwaffe were confiscated after the surrender of Italy in September 1943. In fact, the *Transportgeschwadern* had suffered so many losses in Crete and on the Eastern Front, that the Luftwaffe had to incorporate a few transports supplied by Italy. In late 1942, Italy provided some Savoia Marchetti *Marsupiale* SM 82 which were flown by the 'Savoia Staffel'. This photo was taken on the Cretan airfield of Heraklion at the end of 1942 during the dramatic retreat of the German-Italian troops from Egypt. It shows '1Z + BX', a typical example of the Savoia Staffel with a white band painted on the rear.
(J-L. Roba)

Left: Nightfighters were scarce in the Mediterranean area. From February to October 1941, 1./NJG 3 operated over the desert, and in November 1941, I./NJG 2 was transferred to the Mediterranean. The Gruppe remained in Sicily and Crete until August 1942 before returning to Belgium. But in November, the whole Geschwader was called south to support Panzerarmee Afrika. This Ju 88C-6, coded 'R4 + FR', was photographed on a Sicilian airfield. It is believed to have been flown by Oblt. Hans Rökker, one of the Luftwaffe's best nightfighter pilots and an eventual holder of the Knight's Cross. Notice the complicated camouflage, the *Englandblitz* insignia and the antenna of the FuG 202 Lichtenstein B-C radar, used for nightfighting. I./NJG 2 was used against night bombers, as escort for transport planes and to attack shipping and submarines.
(via J-P Van Mol)

Right: In 1942, 6./KG 26 operated as torpedo bombers against shipping in the Black Sea. But, in October of that year, its He 111s were hurriedly sent to Catania (Sicily). From here the Staffel made night bombing attacks on La Valetta harbour and the three Malta airfields. By day, the crews were also engaged in torpedo attacks against Allied convoys in the central and eastern Mediterranean. Here a machine of 6./KG 26 is seen from another, while on exercise over Sicily.
(Walter Fuss)

Left: KG 60 is often forgotten in Luftwaffe histories. Indeed, the Geschwader had only one Gruppe and a very short life of around six months. I./KG 60 was created in September 1942 to operate in northern Europe, but in November 1942 was transferred south to try and protect the retreat of Panzerarmee Afrika. I./KG 60 was disbanded in February 1943, its resources being given to KG 30 and KG 6. Shown here is Ju 88A-4 'P1 + ??' after having collided with an obstacle on a Sardinian airfield. In the background, an Italian Savoia SM 79 of 255 Squadriglia.
(Alessandru Ragatzu)

CHAPTER TWELVE

In the West, 1941–1942

Since my childhood, I dreamed of piloting large planes; and from my adolescence, I flew gliders, a sport that the Hitler Youth made very popular in Germany. I volunteered for the Luftwaffe in 1940 to avoid being posted to another arm. After several tests, I was accepted in October. I started ground training and began flying school afterwards. I gained my A and B (light planes) certificates while simultaneously studying officer courses. I was taught the C certificate (multi-engined) at Kolberg. When I finally received this certificate, I studied blind flying. In 1942, I gained every possible certificate and was able to pilot all the Luftwaffe's planes in all meteorological conditions. I was then posted to Stab IV./KG 40 based at Chateaudun and I became the Kommandeur's (Major Hemme) Adjutant. We flew Ju 88C-6s fitted with an impressive armament (concentrated in the nose): two 2cm cannons and four machine-guns. Our missions were to escort our U-boats over the Atlantic in order to protect them as long as they were within the Beaufighter and Mosquito radius of action. Indeed, the submarines generally navigated on the surface and their protection against aerial attacks was inadequate. Our principal operational area was in the Bay of Biscay; nevertheless we often flew further towards the south-west and to the northern coast of Spain. We usually performed these kind of missions with four to six aircraft. Our opponents had no combat superiority and our morale was excellent as we knew that, in combat, the winner would be the best crew (there being no technical advantage). The usual Beaufighter and Mosquitos were not our sole opponents: we sometimes had to face torpedo-flying boats and later 'Flying Fortresses'. I claimed my first victory against one of those B-17s.

(Oblt. Lothar Wolf)

Right: **Bernay, at the beginning of 1941. Dr. Carl Hofner, the Medical Officer of III./JG 2 walks away from the snow-covered runway wearing the typical Luftwaffe winter jacket. Behind is an *Emil* of 8./JG 2 as well as an FW 58 *Weihe* coded 'RC+ NE'. This versatile twin-engined machine was often used over the Channel to search for downed aviators.**

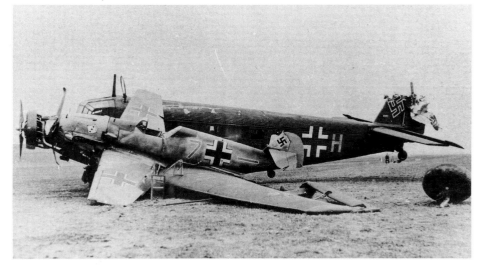

Above: **On 25 April 1941, Uffz. Richard Klapp of 2./EJG 3 (the training unit of JG 3), attempted to land his Bf 109E 'Red 7' at this airfield at Cracovia (Poland). Unfortunately, a group of Ju 52s arriving from Küstrin had the same idea. Ofw. Wilfert, the pilot of one of the three-engined planes, was approaching the airfield below the level of the Bf 109. And Klapp, looking in front of him, didn't keep an eye on what was happening underneath. The final result is apparent from the photo. The unfortunate young fighter pilot was court-martialled, although he was only placed under arrest for three weeks. The incident did not hinder his military career, however, as he ended the war in SG 77. After the war, he joined the reformed West German Luftwaffe.**

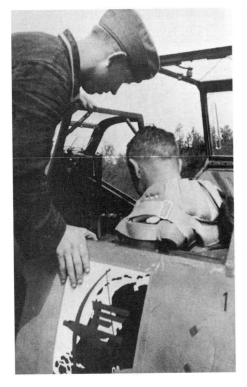

Above: On 9 August 1941, Obstlt. Adolf Galland won his 80th victory. His 81st and 82nd followed quickly (and the bars are just visible on the rudder of his Bf 109E). Also visible are the shield bearing 'S' for Schlageter (the honour name of JG 26) and a Mickey-Mouse badge (Galland's personal insignia). With the *Schwerte* (swords) added on 21 June 1941 to the *Eichenlaub* (oak leaves) and to the *Ritterkreuz*, he became the most decorated officer in the Wehrmacht. By the time he left the command of JG 26 to become General der Jagdflieger (General of the Fighter Pilots), his tally had reached 94 victories (all won in the West). After falling out of favour with Hitler, he eventually returned to the front at the command of JV 44 (an élite unit equipped with the Me 262 jet fighter) where he won another 7 victories.

Above: At the beginning of the war, the Stab of JG 1 controlled several small separate fighter units protecting the German Bight, a vital region with its harbours. As the danger grew from RAF bombers the defences had to be improved, and the Stab was increased to Gruppe strength. The command of the new I. Gruppe was given to Major Dr. Erich Mix in the summer of 1941 (shown here sitting in his Bf 109F). Notice the unit emblem.

Below: 2./JG 1 was the last Staffel of I./JG 1 to be formed, created from a nucleus of pilots of the *Tagjagdstaffel Loddenheide*. Occupying the airfield at Loddenheide (near Münster) then later one at Düsseldorf, the unit was renamed 2./JG 1 upon its arrival at Katwijk (Netherlands) in mid-July 1941. This Bf 109E of the *Tagjagdstaffel Loddenheide* is photographed sheltering under camouflage nets at Düsseldorf in June 1941, a couple of days before its departure to the Netherlands.

Right: The *Emils* of JG 26 were progressively replaced by the *Friedrich* during spring 1941, the new type offering a temporary technical superiority over the RAF's fighters. Shown here is a Bf 109F of 8./JG 26 *Adamsonstaffel*, easily recognizable by the Staffel emblem under the cockpit. This is an early F, with the *Emil*-type supercharger air intake, perhaps an F-0 or F-1.

Left: At the end of summer 1941, II./JG 26 received some FW 190A-1s. This robust and fast aircraft outclassed the Bf 109 in many areas, including speed and dive speed, although its extra weight handicapped it at high altitude. EJG 26 (the training Gruppe of JG 26) based at Wevelgem (Belgium) also received some FW 190s. Here, one of the first to be delivered (and still carrying its factory codes 'SB + IG') sits beside an 'old' Bf 109E.

Right: An Arado 196 taxies in St Nazaire harbour at the end of 1940 or in 1941. This float plane still wears the *Stammkennzeichen* 'DH + HS' and has a very unusual yellow band all around the fuselage. It probably belonged to 5.Bordflieger Staffel, a unit which operated over the Atlantic in a reconnaissance and anti-shipping role. The Ar 196 was a sturdy aircraft which could do surprisingly well against enemy fighters.
(via Rèmy Chuinard)

Left: Beaumont-Le-Roger, early 1941. After the winter lull, pilots and aircraft of JG 2 *Richthofen* prepare for new battles with the RAF. Even so, the beginning of the year sees the progressive move east of the majority of the fighter units, as German attention turns to the Soviet Union. But JG 2 and JG 26 will stay in France, left to deal with the ever-increasing intrusions of the British. Here, pilots of II./JG 2 scramble, helped by their mechanics.
(Ph Hahn)

Left: KG 2 *Holzhammer* was one of the first units to receive the Do 217 in place of their Do 17Zs. In January 1941, 6./KG 2 began training on the new aircraft. The other Staffeln of II./KG 2 also re-equipped for operations over Britain while the rest of the unit was engaged in the East. In October 1941, the whole Geschwader was recalled to the West and completely equipped with the new aircraft, which became a common intruder in the British skies.

Right: Summer 1941, and some of the Bf 109F-2s of 3./JG 2 sit at their dispersal area.

Below and above: One of the most succesful German nightfighter units was without doubt NJG 1, the first of its kind. I./NJG 1 ('G9 + KK' was a 2. Staffel plane) operated mainly from the Low Countries (from Venlo and Deelen), scoring many victories over bombers *en route* to or from northern Germany. II./NJG 1 was transferred to the Belgian airfield of St Truiden and the two Gruppen operated separately, each having its own 'territory'.

Above: The concept of the *Ferne Nachtjagd* (the long-range nightfighter or intruder) was devised from the end of 1940. In September of that year, II./NJG 1 was redesignated I./NJG 2 (with the code 'R4'). Its Ju 88Cs operated over British airfields trying to catch the RAF bombers taking off or landing by night. One year later, the unit claimed its 142nd victory, but was recalled to defend the Reich's territory. It was decided that it was more important to preserve the morale of the civilian population by bringing the wreckage down on German soil. This Ju 88C-4, apparently on a Dutch airfield in 1941, is presumed to have been the machine of Hptm. Karl Hülshoff's, the unit's Kommandeur.
(J-P. Van Mol)

Left: The pilot of this machine (possibly from ZG 76, note the shark's mouth) has painted on his Bf 110 the flags of all the nations where he has fought. Presumably photographed in the winter of 1941–42, the aircraft shows the flags of Belgium, France, Britain, the Netherlands, Greece, Iraq, Yugoslavia, Norway and Denmark. A comprehensive career, proving that the Geschwader was engaged on all fronts from 1939 (although not in Poland).
(Wilhelm Becker)

Right: On 12 February 1942, the German battleships *Scharnhorst*, *Gneisenau* and *Prinz Eugen* left the French harbour of Brest to sail northwards. They had to pass through the Channel, running the gauntlet of probable RAF attacks. To protect the ships, the Luftwaffe created an airborne umbrella of fighters which followed the convoy from Brittany to Norway. Nightfighters were also used. Here, at the end of the journey, Bf 110s of II./NJG 1 fly over the Norwegian mountains. This unit was based at St. Trond (Belgium) but had to protect the ships along the coasts of Belgium, the Netherlands and Scandinavia. The insignia of the *Nachtjagd* is clearly visible. Also visible are the codes 'G9 + LN' and 'G9 + FM': all planes of the 5th Staffel.
(Hannes Forke)

Left: In February 1942, the combat Staffel of No.1 Fighter School (Einsatzstaffel der JFS 1) was sent to Norway in order to reinforce the units committed to *Operation Donnerkeil* (the movement north of the Kriegsmarine's capital ships). Placed under the command of Hptm. Fritz Losigkeit, several Bf 109Es and Fs flew combat patrols around the big ships. This Bf 109F (with Oblt. Friedrich Eberle sitting on the wheel) carries the school's emblem.

Above: The Kapitän of the Einsatzstaffel der JFS 1, Oblt. Friedrich Eberle, gained his first combat experience with JG 51 during the Battle of Britain, where he claimed 12 victories. The use of his unit for *Donnerkeil* gave him the chance to return to the front, and with several other officers (among them Hptm. Fritz Losigkeit) committed briefly to Norway, he formed the core of a new fighter Gruppe. Created in April 1942, it was baptised IV./JG 1. Eberle received the command of the 10. Staffel. Note on his Bf 109E-7 'White 1' (WNr. 6412) the circle behind the *Balkenkreuz*, a marking reserved for the IVth Gruppen.

Above: The order to form NJG 4 was given in January 1941 but a year passed before the effective creation of the nightfighter unit. III./NJG 4 was formed in May 1942 with 1., 4. and 8./NJG 1. This Bf 110, '3C + DS' of 8./NJG 4, is the mount of Lt. Ludwig Meister, who arrived a few months earlier from 5./NJG 1, and was transferred to the new unit after claiming three victories. Flying in the main with his wireless operator, Fw. Hannes Forke, Meister went on to be credited with 38 bombers, operating later in I./NJG 4 and finally coming back as Kommandeur of III./NJG 4. He was awarded the *Ritterkreuz* in June 1944 and survived the war.
(Ludwig Meister)

Above: Taken during a transit flight or daytime exercise, this photo shows Bf 110s of 9./NJG 1. It presumably dates from the beginning of 1942 when the nightfighters were Bf 110Cs wearing black camouflage. Notice the hardly visible grey fuselage codes (the aircraft in the foreground is 'G9 + DT').
(J-L. Roba)

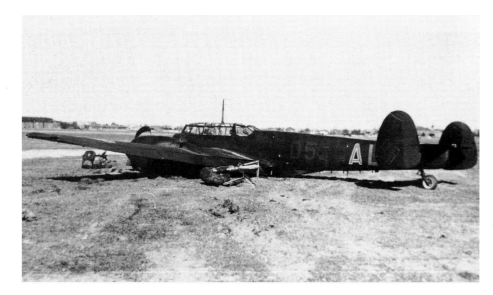

Left and below: In 1942, returning from a night mission, Lt. Hans Meyer (2./NJG 3), had to belly-land his Bf 110C 'D5 + AL' (from the 3rd Staffel) on the Dutch airfield of Venlo. Notice that the individual letter 'A' was painted on the nose, under the guns. Meyer claimed one victory over the Netherlands but also survived a number of crashes. In mid-1943, he was transferred to IV./NJG 6 in Romania, and became Staffelkapitän of 10./NJG 6 in 1944. He scored two victories there before returning to Germany. At the end of the war he was trained on the Me 262 jet.
(Hans Meyer)

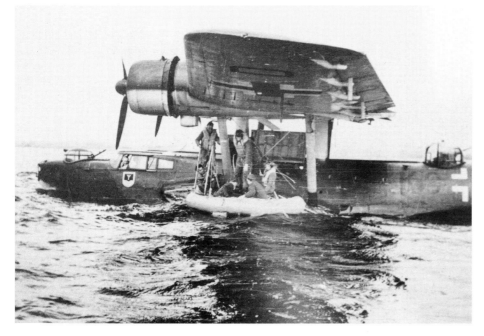

Left: A rescue exercise for 'KO + ?D', one of the Do 24s of 4. Seenotstaffel based at Norderney. The photo clearly shows the two turrets with their defensive armament. This flying boat was liked by its crews for its sturdiness and ability to shoot it out with attacking fighters.
(J-L. Roba)

Right: **Hptm. Wilhelm Herget flew in the beginning of the war in II./ZG 76, operating in Western Europe and in Iraq (1941). When he was transferred to the nightfighters, he decided to keep the shark mouth insignia on his Bf 110. Shown here is his machine '3C + ET' parked on a French airfield (Athis or Juvincourt) in 1942. At that time, Herget was Kommandeur of II./NJG 4, although he seems have flown with a 9.Staffel aircraft. Credited with 73 victories (58 by night),** *Ritterkreuzträger* **Herget died in 1974.**
(Roland Charlier)

Left: **At the end of May 1942, JG 2 received its first FW 190A-2s. Shown here is 'Black 11' of 2./JG 2.**

Right: **By the summer of 1942, only 11. Staffel of JG 2 is still equipped with Bf 109s. This is a special high-altitude squadron flying G-1s fitted with a pressurised cockpit. Shown here is the Staffelkapitän, Oblt. Julius Meimberg, as he leaves 'White 11'. At this time Meimberg has 20 victories to his credit, all won in the West.**

Left: Scramble for the pilots of 7./JG 2, who run toward their FW 190s (A-2s or A-3s). In the foreground, the indispensable *Anlasswagen* (a hand-drawn battery cart needed to start the FW 190). Note the dark decoration behind the exhaust, possibly meant to hide the discolouring caused by the exhaust gasses. The Staffel emblem is just visible on the cowling of 'White 6'.

Right: In January 1942, JG 1 was given a IIIrd Gruppe. Its principal missions were to protect Denmark and the southern coasts of Norway. Its pilots flew tiring and dangerous missions above the North Sea, almost without any contact with the RAF. Equipped with Bf 109Es (here an E-7 of 7./JG 1), the Gruppe eventually changed to FW 190s towards the end of spring 1942.

Left: On 21 August 1942, Ofw. Detlev Lüth and his comrades of II./JG 1 encountered for the first time four-engined American bombers in their defensive formations or 'boxes'. Astonished by the strength of the defensive fire, the Germans launched only a few attacks. No kills were achieved, and worse, Lüth had to belly-land his FW 190A-2 (WNr. 2116) near Katwijk. German flyers quickly learned how best to deal with the American formations, however, and devised various tactics, especially that of frontal attacks. Lüth became an expert against the *Viermots* (four-engined aircraft) but was killed on 6 March 1944 during the first large daylight raid on Berlin.

Above: Probably the most renowned German nightfighter unit was II./NJG 1 based at the Belgian airfield of St Trond (St Truiden) and nicknamed 'The St Trond Ghosts'. This black Bf 110 was manned in 1942 by Lt. Hans Autenrieth, who gained many victories over Belgium and France. He always flew with Uffz. Adam (shown holding the MG 15 machine gun), the radio operator with whom he teamed up at nightfighter school. Notice the white 'II' near the nightfighter insignia (the *Englandblitz*) indicating that the plane belongs to II Gruppe, and the aerial mast (*Antennen Anpassungsgerät*), part of the radio navigation system. This crew was transferred to III./NJG 4 in 1943, and was shot down in June 1944 near Fougères (France) while operating against the D-Day landings. Both were captured by the French Resistance. Adam was shot and officially listed as missing, but Autenrieth was lucky enough to be handed over to an American unit as a POW. He died in 1996.
(Hans Autenrieth)

Above: Lt. Wilhelm-Ferdinand Galland was posted to Abbeville on 27 June 1941, to the Geschwader commanded by his famous brother Adolf. He was a gifted pilot in his own right, scoring his first victory on 23 July. On 5 May 1942 (by which time he had scored eight kills) he became Staffelkapitän of 5./JG 26. In this photo, taken in the spring of 1942, he seems in pensive mood, examining the damage to the rudder of his FW 190A-3 (WNr. 230). Eventually reaching the rank of major, *Wutz* Galland was shot down and killed over Belgium during the first large raid on Schweinfurt, on 17 August 1943. By then his tally was 55 victories (among them eight four-engined bombers and 37 Spitfires).

Left: **Hptm. Hans *Assi* Hahn was an ace who flew with JG 2. After becoming Kommandeur of III./JG 2 with 68 victories won in the West, he took command in November 1942 of II./JG 54 on the Eastern Front. In three months, he claimed 40 new victories before being shot down and captured. He survived the captivity and returned to Germany at the end of 1949. He is seen here at St. Pol, just after leaving JG 2's *Storch*, often used by fighter pilots to visit the crash sites of their victims.**

Above: **This Fi 156 *Storch* wears the *Englandblitz* on the nose and the code 'CK + KF'. It was a liaison machine belonging to NJG 1.**

Right: **Autumn 1942. Taxiing toward the dispersal area, this FW 190A-3 'Yellow 5' of 7./JG 1 dropped its left wheel into a drainage gully. The propeller blades were twisted while hitting the ground.**

Below left and right: **FW 200** *Condor* **'F8 + CH' of I./KG 40 flies over the Atlantic in search of enemy shipping. The photo probably dates from the end of 1942. Soon the unit will leave Bordeaux-Merignac to be sent to the East (at the time of the Stalingrad encirclement) before being re-equipped with He 177s. 'F8 + CH' does not carry the unit's crest, unlike the other** *Condor* **seen here in the hands of the ground crew.**
(J-L. Roba)

CHAPTER THIRTEEN

Norway, 1942

On 10 May 1942 at 15.50hr, we started with eight Bf 110s from Kirkenes to escort a Stuka group flying to Murmansk. The Stukas aborted their mission, turning back over Liza when they sighted to the north a Soviet bomber group (around seven SB-3s) flying over the Notowki Bight under large escort (15–20 MiGs and Hurricanes). They flew at 2800 meters to the west. Our Staffel immediately dived on the enemy group but the escort prevented us from attacking their bombers: the dogfight began. In the meantime, we could observe the enemy bombers jettisoning their bombs and turning back. Already on the first attack, Oblt. Karl-Fritz Schloßstein (5th victory) and Ofw. Munding (4th) shot down a MiG-3 and a Hurricane. A Rotte (pair) of MiGs attacked a Hs 123 flying over the western bank of the Riza, and Ofw. Theo Weißenberger shot them both down in two attacks (14th and 15th victories). In the meantime, some of our Bf 110s followed several Soviets trying to escape towards the east and Ofw. Rudolf Kurpiers shot down a Hurricane and a MiG-3 (1st and 2nd victories). The other fighters remained very close to the bombers, protecting them. North-west of the Liza Bight, Ofw. Theo Weißenberger and Reinhold Fiedler destroyed two Hurricanes, the planes falling into the sea. The enemy then took the Ura Bight direction followed by our aircraft.

Ofw. Theo Weißenberger claimed his 17th and 18th victories (one Hurricane and one MiG-3) and three more were claimed by our pilots. In total: seven Hurricanes and six MiG-3s were reported shot down. Our damage was four hits on a Bf 110, but nothing serious.

(Oblt. Karl-Fritz Schloßstein, Stk. of 10.(Z)/JG 5)

Above: **Staffelkapitän of 6.(Z)/JG 5 (formerly 1.(Z)/JG 77), Oblt. Felix-Maria Brandis is playing with the unit mascots, Herdla and Lockheed. On 2 February 1942, he was killed in his Bf 110E-2, crashing near Olanga in poor visibility, and becoming the first casualty in his unit. His radio operator, Fw. Herbert Baus, was lightly wounded.**

Right: **Two Bf 110s ('LN + AR' and 'LN + TR') of 13.(Z)/JG 5 (formerly 6.(Z)/JG 5) overfly Kirkenes Fjord during the spring of 1942.**

Above and right: **After having led 7./JG 54 on the Russian Front, Hptm. Günther Scholz was appointed Gruppenkommandeur of III./JG 5, a unit created in January 1942. From April, this Gruppe was based in Petsamo (Finland) from where it launched numerous missions against the harbour at Murmansk and on the *Murmanbahn*, the railway linking the port to the rest of the Soviet Union. In August 1942, the Kommandeur gained his 30th kill. He is seen here on his victorious return to the airfield.**

Above: **This Bf 109F 'Black 10' of 8./JG 5 was shot down over Murmansk by Soviet AA on 26 December 1942. Captured unhurt, Uffz. Josef Kaiser managed to persuade his jailers that he was a Communist sympathiser, by showing a document proving that his brother belonged to the Austrian Communist party. After being trained for several weeks as a radio-operator, Kaiser was parachuted behind German lines in the summer of 1943 to spy for the Russians. He immediately gave himself up to the German authorities. He wasn't the only such case – two JG 77 pilots were also captured and dropped as spies behind German lines in 1942. They too surrendered to their compatriots.**

Below: **Ofw. Rudolf Müller (here climbing out of a Bf 109 bearing his personal insignia) was the most successful pilot of II./JG 5 in 1942. Having gained his first victory in September 1941 (during his third combat mission), he reached 46 kills on 17 June 1942 and was awarded the *Ritterkreuz*. At the end of the year, he had around 80 victories. He was shot down on 19 April 1943, and captured a few days later after being picked up by a Soviet patrol. He seems to have died in Soviet captivity but one source claims that he lived until the 1990s, after a long career as a flying instructor in the USSR.**

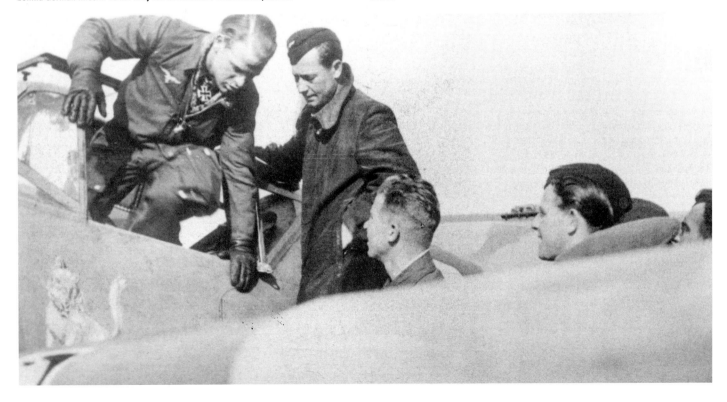

Right: **Another view of Bf 109F 'Yellow 3' of 6./JG 5, the machine belonging to the ace Ofw. Rudolf Müller.**

Left: **A II./JG 5 *Storch* photographed in North Finland in 1942. This machine was flown by Lt. Wulf Widowitz, who specialized in rescuing German pilots shot down in the tundra. Quite a few pilots were saved in these difficult and dangerous missions.**

Right: **Norway provided a base for German bombers, who flew against the Allied convoys bringing supplies of war material to the Red Army via Murmansk. The photograph shows a formation of He 111Hs of an unknown unit. (Manfred Griehl)**

CHAPTER FOURTEEN

USSR, 1943–44

I flew in my transport squadron on many fronts (Balkans, Russian) and I faced many difficult situations. But the most striking operation was without doubt the Stalingrad pocket. This time we had to bring in no more soldiers, but to save the maximum number of men from capture or death. Their only hope was the aerial bridge as the city was encircled for many weeks and the living conditions were frightening. Despite all the efforts of our mechanics, we could fly only a handful of planes and it was obvious from the beginning that we could save only a small part of the encircled garrison. The last airfield that we could use in the Stalingrad area was Pitomnik. I landed there two times. To avoid being shot by Soviet planes, we flew only by night.

On 8 January 1943, I took off from Salk at 19.40hr and landed my heavy three-engined transport on the tiny and snowy landing ground two hours later. To improve visibility for our meagre rescue planes, the airfield was illuminated in the faint hope of seeing the transports landing. The frost covered the ground and hindered the braking and manoeuvring; it was a great feat to make a good landing. The sight before our eyes was awful: long files of wounded soldiers, on the edge of the airfield, left without protection against the snow or the bitter wind. The frost was so heavy that we could stop the two exterior engines for only 20 minutes. Above that time, the oil solidified and it became impossible to start again. While the material was unloaded and the wounded loaded, only the middle engine turned and maintained the battery to restart the two stopped engines. The wounded were almost thrown in the plane and we took off again when the fuselage was full. On that day (8 January 1943), my Ju 52 suffered some technical troubles and I could start only at 23.00hr. In the air, the temperature was -40 degrees but nevertheless the crew members gave their fur jackets to cover the wounded. When the 'passengers' were unloaded in Salk, I discovered that the situation was worse than I imagined . . . The bandages were full of lice; the fuselage was stained with blood . . . The following day, I made my second and last mission to Pitomnik (starting at 15.45hr and landing at 18.30hr). This time all went faster and, after 15 minutes, I took off with my load of suffering, landing at Salk at 21.30hr. From the 10th, our Tante Ju could not land any more on the tiny Pitomnik airfield and we were sent to Basagino. One week later, there was another change, the landing ground of Saparoske being our new destination.
(Walter Waldenberger, 3./KGzbV 1)

Above and below: **Summer clothes, winter clothes… Fw. Walter Waldenberger photographed some of his crewmen in front of their Ju 52 '1Z + FL' of 3./KGzbV 1. In winter, the all-green three-engined transport was covered with temporary washable white paint. In the summer, the black letters were outlined in white; in winter, the yellow 'F' (the individual letter) was outlined in black over a yellow band (painted nearer the cross for some reason). With this aircraft, Waldenberger flew two supply missions to Pitomnik (Stalingrad), returning each time with a plane-load of wounded soldiers.**
(Walter Waldenberger)

Above: To supply the Stalingrad pocket, the Luftwaffe organized an aerial bridge using all available Ju 52 transport units. To supplement their numbers, Luftflotte 4 used He 111 units, namely KGzbV 5 and 20, KG 27 and 55, III./KG 4 and I./KG 100. The wreckage of this He 111 (WNr. 4975) is shown at the beginning of 1943, after the city was in Soviet hands. It was probably destroyed at Pitomnik. The *Stammkennzeichen* (factory delivery codes) '??+ML' can be seen under the unit codes '??+BA' which have been quickly applied over the washable winter white paint. This implies that the aircraft had only just been delivered to its unit before being destroyed.

Above: Not all transport aircraft were formed into Geschwader, some were assigned to transport groups. This was the case with TGr. 30, raised in March 1943 and equipped with He 111s. Shown here is 'S3 + LL' of the 3rd Staffel, on a snowy airfield in the USSR towards the end of March 1943. In the last months of the war, the Gruppe was very active in supplying German 'pockets' (such as Dunkirk and Royan) cut off by the advancing Allies on the Atlantic coast.

Above: Early 1943, and Ju 88A-4 '5K + DK' of 2./KG 3 has belly-landed on the airfield at Charkow-Woitschenko. The port-side propeller has been ripped off by the impact on the frozen ground.
(Jochen Menke)

97

Left: **An unidentified Ju87 *Stuka* in the Russian winter.**

Right: **Seen from the rear, this FW 189A2 of 1.(H)/31 shows the white camouflage used in winter time. The washable paint has nearly disappeared under the harsh weather conditions.**

Left: **A pristine white Bf 110E carrying the code '8H' and belonging to 4.(H)/Aufklärungsgruppe 33. This unit was raised in the spring of 1941 for the attack on Russia with four independent Staffeln. In the beginning of 1942 2. and 4.(F)/33 were renamed 2. and 4.(H)/33. 4.(H)/33 flew mainly in the northern (in NAG 13 and NAG 8) and southern (in NAG 12) part of the front.**

In 1944, the Staffel was equipped with Bf 109s and received the name 3./NAG 14. Under this name the unit then operated in the Balkans, retreating slowly back to the Reich.

Above left: **In February 1943, I./JG 54 was recalled to Heiligenbeil to re-equip with the FW 190. The pilots were generally pleased with this change as the FW 190 had better performance and was much tougher than the Bf 109; an important consideration when facing Soviet AA defences in the Leningrad area.**

Above right: **One of the least-known German transport aircraft is without doubt the Ar 232. This machine, with its 'modern' shape, was only produced in low numbers (around 50). It was nicknamed *Tausendfüsser* (millipede) or *Tatzelwurm* (a mythical Alpine dragon) as it had 22 wheels to keep the ground pressure low. It could even taxi across narrow trenches! Notice the glazed nose and the height of the tail booms. Ar 232s were engaged in the Stalingrad aerial bridge, and legend has it that the prototype V2 was the last machine to leave the pocket. A handful of Ar 232Bs (the four-engined version) were used by KG 200 in *Operation Zeppelin*, an unsuccessful attempt to assassinate Marshal Stalin in September 1944.**

Right: **On 20 February 1943, I./JG 54 left the Leningrad front to participate in the great battles above Stalingrad. During the first three days of the battle, I./JG 54 claimed dozens of victories. Its leader, Major Hans Philipp, one of the greatest aces, claimed seven victories on 23 February alone. On 17 March, he became the second pilot in history to reach a score of 200 victories. Posted to the West a few days after this, he was finally killed in action as Kommodore of JG 1 on 8 October 1943.**

Left and below: **In January 1943, the pilots of I./JG 26 were pleased to hear that they would replace III./JG 54 on the Eastern Front. The Soviet Air Forces had a poor reputation, and most pilots saw this as an opportunity to increase their personal tally. From the end of January I./JG 26 was based on the airfield at Rielbitzi where the situation was quiet. In June, the unit was called back to France. The photographs show aircraft of 2./JG 26 in the USSR in the spring of 1943.**

Left: **French Gnome-Rhone engines were extensively used by the Luftwaffe. They powered the Hs 129 and the Me 323 (the motorised version of the Me 321 glider). If six engines were needed for the Me 323, only two were necessary for the Go 244, the motorised version of the Go 242 glider. Shown here is '4V + BP' of KGzbV. 106 on a German airfield. The conversion was not a great success, the aircraft being extremely vulnerable to enemy fire. Only a few were made.**
(J-L. Roba)

Above, left and right: The Me 321 transport glider was so large that a single aircraft could not tow it. The Germans developed two solutions. First was the *troika*; three Bf 110s taking off in formation, each with a cable attached to the glider. The danger of collision or of cables tangling was very high. The second solution was the He 111Z *Zwilling* (twins). Two normal He 111s were joined by a centre wing section holding a fifth engine, the whole combination manned by a crew in the port fuselage. Shown here is He 111Z 'DG + DY' with the Eastern Front yellow fuselage band. Only a small number of He 111Zs were built, as the Me 321 was given its own engines to become the Me 323.
(J-L. Roba)

Above: An autonomous fighter unit known as *Oelschutzstaffel Ploesti* was created in early 1942 to protect the vital Romanian oil installations at Ploesti. Several pilots of III./JG 77 were posted to the new unit, such as Fw. Albert Palm, a successful pilot who claimed 23 victories in Russia.

Left: In the summer of 1942, *Oelschutzstaffel Ploesti* was integrated into the newly formed I./JG 4, and remained based at Mizil, close to the oil installations, until November 1943. This Gruppe was successful on its first combat with enemy bombers, when on 1 August 1943 it intercepted the American raid on Ploesti. Several Bf 109G-2s are seen here. Note the yellow strip after the *Balkenkreuz.*

Right: Taganrog, in the summer of 1943. Oberst Pzcil sits in his Bf 109G-2, which bears the double chevron and the Staffel insignia of 15.(Kroatische)/JG 52. Standing close to the wing is Lt. Dragustin Ivanic. The Croatian Staffel was included in III./JG 52 in late 1941. In 1942, 13.(Slowakische)/JG 52 was also integrated in the Gruppe. Both units operated with III./JG 52 until the end of 1943.

Left: Russian Front, southern sector, spring 1943. A Bf 109G of 2./JG 52 with two 20mm MG 151 cannon in underwing gondolas. Under the cockpit is the well-known sword of JG 52, and on the engine cowling, the insignia of 2./JG 52.

Above: On 5 November 1942, at the age of 20, Lt. Erich Hartmann of 7./JG 52 won his first victory. This *Abschuss* was not remarkable at the time, as JG 52 had racked up an amazing score of kills. One of the pilots, Oblt. Gerhard Barkhorn, even claimed his 100th personal success on 19 December 1942. But Hartmann went on to score 100 of his own by September 1943 – and he didn't stop there. He reached 200 on 2 March 1944; and on 23 August, he shot down his 300th aircraft! Barkhorn kept up though, and became the second pilot to reach 300, at the end of 1944. Hartmann (352 claims in total) and Barkhorn (301) survived the war.

Left and above: In the winter of 1943–1944, Oblt. Hans Wolf, a pilot in 2./ZG 76, celebrates his 100th combat mission. Notice the crude application of the temporary white paint, the large markings and the coloured outline around the code letters and fuselage cross. Strangely, the codes 'A5' are not those of ZG 76 but of St.G. 1. Wolf left the unit in February 1944 and later joined II.(Sturm)/JG 4.
(Hans Wolf)

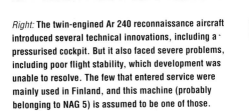

Left: The asymmetrical Blohm und Voss BV 141 reconnaissance aircraft was one of the strangest-looking machines flown by the Luftwaffe. Its unusual shape (engine and tail boom on one side, cockpit nacelle on the other) is more appreciated today by modellers than it was by the original crews. This idiosyncratic design was considered to be underpowered and difficult to fly, and was only produced in small numbers. It saw service mainly on the Eastern Front.

Right: The twin-engined Ar 240 reconnaissance aircraft introduced several technical innovations, including a pressurised cockpit. But it also faced severe problems, including poor flight stability, which development was unable to resolve. The few that entered service were mainly used in Finland, and this machine (probably belonging to NAG 5) is assumed to be one of those.

Left: In October 1943, II./SKG 10 was redesignated II./SG 4. The unit operated alongside I./SG 4 in Italy but at the end of the year transferred to the East to operate against Soviet ground forces in the northern sector of the front. After a short interlude in the West (for the Battle of the Bulge), II./SG 4 came back to operate in Hungary and Silesia. FW 190G-3 'White S' of 4./SG 4 was photographed during these operations, possibly around February 1945. Note the green/white propeller spinner and the bombs in the foreground.
(J-L. Roba)

Right and below: **During 1944, Schlachtgeschwader 10 was heavily engaged in many of the key battles on the Eastern Front. This FW 190 of I./SG 10 is shown being maintained, possibly on a Romanian airfield. Note that the fighter still wears its** *Stammkennzeichen* **(delivery codes), apparently 'KS + ME'.**
(Werner Zirus)

Right: **After the fall of Yugoslavia in April 1941, a bitter and vicious conflict continued, with German troops and their allies fighting partisan groups. The Luftwaffe provided a few small units to support the ground troops, often equipped with a variety of obsolete machines.**

The Ju 87 *Stuka* **was perhaps the most modern aircraft available, and a Staffel is seen here flying over the Bosnian mountains searching for a target. Flying over the Balkans was a dangerous task, with terrain and weather posing numerous difficulties. The partisans could also shoot at low-flying aircraft, and if a downed flyer was captured he could usually expect to be killed.**
(J-L. Roba)

CHAPTER FIFTEEN

The Mediterranean, 1943–1944

On 12 July 1943, take off of three Ju 52s of 11. Staffel ('P3 B', 'P3 C' and 'P3 J') under the command of Ofw. Mayer with a load of radio material and twelve Luftwaffe personnel. Destination was Catania. Following orders, we landed at 09.15hr at Vibo Valentia to be escorted by fighters. The Kommandeur of the Pik-As unit told us that, following the enemy situation, no escort was needed. We then took off at 11.00hr to Catania airfield. We did not receive authorization to land. We were then surprised by two Spitfires. They attacked 'P3 B' which was set on fire but could make an emergency landing 50m south of the airfield. The second Spitfire attack on 'P3 C' forced it to land in a hurry, 3 km W. of the airfield. When 'P3 J' tried to land, a Spitfire attacked it twice without hitting it. The air gunners of the three Ju 52 returned fire but it seems that no enemy was touched

Losses: Ju 52 'P3 B' totally destroyed (by fire); Crewmen: Fw. Ulber (pilot) and Uffz. Nowack (Flight Engineer) severely burnt (loaded in 'P3 J' to be brought to Ciampino-Nord and treated in the Lw. Lazarett in Rome).Uffz. Kogler (W/Op.) and Ogfr. Milauf (Air Gunner) killed (burnt). Passengers: four Luftwaffe men killed. Ju 52 'P3 C' crash-landed (ca 60%). Crew and passengers unhurt. Comment of the Staffelführer: if the three Ju 52s had been escorted, the losses could have been avoided.

Report of Uffz. Zamisch (11./TG 1)

Right, above and below: **Scenes in Tunisia. In May 1942, III./JG 53 was deployed to the Mediterranean area to support the German and Italian forces and operate over Malta. The other two Gruppen of the Geschwader followed, in time to take part in the last battles in Africa. The two photos show planes of the *Pik-As* (ace of spades) in Tunisia around March/April 1943. These young Tunisians are examining cannon-equipped Bf 109, while the other picture shows groundcrews reading mail just received from Germany.**
(PK)

Above left: **After it was encircled in the Tunisian pocket, Panzerarmee Afrika needed to fly in all its supplies and reinforcements. The newly created I./KGzbV 323, equipped with the Me 323 motorised glider, was transferred to the theatre at the end of 1942. II./KGzbV 323 followed at the beginning of 1943. On Sunday 22 April 1943, 14 of the six-engined planes were shot down by Allied fighters. The remnants of the two units were then reconstituted as a *Kampfgruppe* before becoming I. and II./TG 5 at the end of April 1943. This picture demonstrates the load-carrying capability of the Me 323, as an eight-wheeled SdKfz. 232 is unloaded on African soil. The aircraft is an Me 323D-2, with French LeO engines and two-bladed propellers.**
(Karl Opitz, via A. Ragatzu)

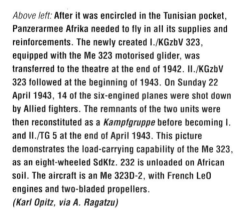

Above right: **I. and II./KGzbV 323 (later TG 5) flew to Africa to bring vehicles, material and reinforcements. On the return journey they were often loaded with wounded men or POWs. This Me 323 has landed at the Italian base of Pomigliano (near Naples) carrying casualties, and is waiting for the ambulances to take them to local hospitals. The aircraft could be 'DT + IG' (WNr. 1207?) which was flown by Oblt. Ernst Peter (who later published his memoirs *Schleppte und Flog Giganten*).**
(Yves Empain)

Right: **Inside a Me 323 flying over the Mediterranean. German soldiers in tropical uniform are assembled in the front of the giant aircraft in the half-darkness. On the left, a man next to a machine gun scans the sky for other aircraft. The Me 323 was easy prey, not only for fighters but even for fast bombers (such as the B-26s who scored some kills against them). Mainly constructed from wood, the ex-glider would quickly catch fire – and of course, smoking was forbidden!**
(PK)

Left: The survival of German troops in Tunisia depended on the aerial bridge whose backbone was the Ju 52 force. Large formations of *Tante Jus* became a common sight in the Mediterranean skies, but they were easy prey for Allied fighters. Here, at least a dozen fly at low level over the sea towards the German-held pocket.

Right: Combat losses in the Mediterranean required a constant flow of replacement aircraft. These two new Bf 109G-6s are probably waiting for better weather before flying over the Alps to Italy, perhaps to Vicenza or to Bari, the delivery point for machines *en route* to Africa. They still have their factory codes ('NP + PO' and 'NP + PH?') but already have a European camouflage and the white band.
(Gerz Family)

Left: With the fighting in Tunisia, all the escort machines in the theatre had to be diverted to the central Mediterranean. This Bf 110D of 3./ZG 26 *Horst Wessel* was photographed on a Sicilian airfield. These twin-engined fighters suffered heavy losses when facing Allied air superiority.
(J-L. Roba)

Right: German mechanics work on the landing gear of a Ju 88A-4 of KG 54, possibly on the Sicilian airfield at Trapani, possibly in January 1943, when the unit was called upon to support German and Italian forces in Tunisia. The *Totenkopf* (death's head) Geschwader had operated for quite some time in the Mediterranean area. In December 1941, Stab and I./KG 54 were deployed to Sicily to operate over Malta (with the help of K.Gr. 606 and 866). In March 1942, IV./KG 54 arrived as reinforcement, and in September 1942 K.Gr.806 became III./KG 54. By that time operations were mainly conducted over North Africa. When the Allies started to bomb the Sicilian airfields, KG 54 had to retreat to the Italian mainland.
(PK)

Below: Allied troops landed on Sicily in the early hours of 10 July 1943, the US 7th Army coming ashore between Licatta and Scoglitti. German fighter units (JG 53 and JG 77) were hastily sent to attack the landing forces. This photo shows American MPs of the first wave inspecting a Bf 109G-6 *Kanonnenboot* of JG 53 (perhaps from 8. Staffel) which has belly-landed on the beach. Records are incomplete, and the machine and pilot cannot be identified. He seems to have survived the crash, although whether or not he became a POW is not known.
(US National Archives)

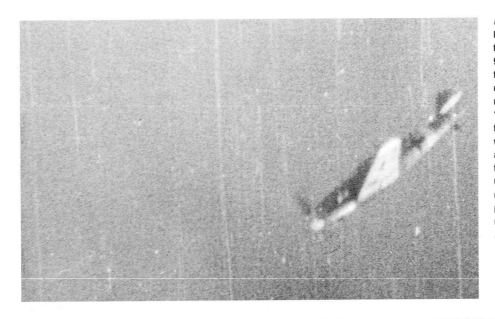

Left and below: **Born in 1923, Hugo Hauck joined the Luftwaffe in the summer of 1940, finishing his training at the EJG at St Jean d'Angely (Western France). Joining 9./JG 77 in Africa in January 1943, the young Leutnant flew around 10 or 12 combat missions before being shot down on 26 February while escorting fighter-bombers near Medenine (Tunisia). The engine of his Bf 109G-6 'Yellow 8' was hit by the fire of a 145 Squadron Spitfire, flown by F/Lt. Ian Shand. Hauck managed to bail out and was captured. He was introduced to the Spitfire pilots, and swapped insignia with Shand. Hauck was then transferred to the USA and remained in captivity in Canada and Britain until April 1947. Recently, Shand (living in Zimbabwe) managed to trace him and send a photo from his gun camera showing the end of 'Yellow 8' more than fifty years earlier.**
(Hugo Hauck)

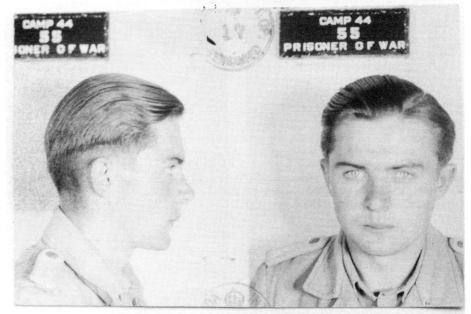

Left: **When the Luftwaffe evacuated African soil in May 1943, one of the last aircraft to leave Tunisia was this 'hack' machine of II./JG 77. Heavily laden with men and equipment, the twin-engined FW 58 took off from Tunis and landed in Sicily. The *Weihe* is photographed here flying alongside the Sicilian coast.**
(Jürgen Puhr-Westerheide)

Right and below: In the final days in North Africa, some Luftwaffe combat units were hastily dispatched to Tunisia. Shown here is a FW 190 fighter-bomber of SG 2, photographed at a repair unit in Tunisia. It carries the Geschwader crest, Mickey Mouse with an axe in his right hand, sitting astride a falling bomb. The close-up shows the same insignia on another aircraft. When SG 2 was incorporated into SG 4, Mickey Mouse became famous in the Italian skies. Note the tropical filter.
(Günther Behling)

Right: In the lead-up to the invasion of Sicily, Allied air forces attacked all the Axis airfields on the island. When the troops landed and captured the area, many destroyed aircraft were found. Shown here are the wrecks of two He 111s captured near Catania. The nearest one has no readable codes, while 'GG + GJ' (probably a hack or transport machine) is in the background. Note the white band and the white wing tips.
(US Air Force)

Right and below: **Transport units of the Luftwaffe suffered heavy losses between Sicily and Africa in their attempts to supply the encircled German ground forces. One of the squadrons hastily sent to the Mediterranean was LTS (Lufttransportstaffel) 290, equipped with Ju 90s and 290s. After flying to Africa, the unit remained in the Mediterranean in support of the German garrisons on Corsica and Sardinia. In the first picture, Ju 90 'J4 + KH' (WNr. 009) is shown flying along the coast of Sardinia in June 1943. The second picture shows 'J4 + JH' (WNr. 007) under attack by American raiders (B-26s?) on 23 July 1943. The four-engined machine (flown by Ofw. Boldt) managed to land on the sea near Bastia (Corsica) but was lost. In September 1943, LTS 290 moved from Italy to Munich-Mühldorf.**
(Müller and US National Archives)

Right: **In mid-1943, I./SG 2 was transferred for some weeks to airfields in Sardinia. The Gruppe was there for a rest period and did not fly many combat missions, although it did suffer from Allied bombing. This FW 190 'Black D' of the 2nd Staffel was photographed at Milis. Notice the simplified markings: a single letter, a fuselage cross and the white band of the Mediterranean theatre.**
(Werner Zirus)

Above: After the departure from Italy of I./SG 2 in August 1943, the *Schlachtgruppe* received some young inexperienced pilots. The *Alte Hase* (experienced pilots) used the unit's FW 44 *Stieglitz* to give extra training to the newcomers. Shown here is 'TM + NM', probably photographed on the Austrian airfield of Graz. *(Werner Zirus)*

Above: To reinforce German defences in the Aegean, the *Zerstörer* Staffel of ZG 26 *Horst Wessel* was transferred to Eleusis airfield, south of Athens. In front of this Ju 88C-6 '3U + WU' of 10./ZG 26, Lt. Regel receives flowers for his 200th combat mission in July 1943. ZG 26 was soon to be engaged in the bloody battles for the Dodecanese islands, losing several crews.

Below: Mechanics working on a FW 190A-7 of Schlachtgeschwader 4 in Italy. This unit was created in October 1943 from Gruppen of SG 2 and the remnants of II. and I I I ./ SKG 10. SG 4 harassed Allied troops in Italy, first being based at Guidonia and, in 1944, in Piacenza/Viterbo. The unit flew many *Jabo* (fighter bomber) missions, often being protected by fighters of I./JG 4, JG 51, JG 53 or JG 77. It was led by some of the great ground attack 'aces', such as Major Heinrich Brücker (Kommodore until May 1944), Hptm. Werner Dörnbrack (Kdr of I./SG 4, then in 1945, Kommodore of the Geschwader), and Hptm. Gerhard Walther (Kdr of I./SG 4, KIA 18 May 1944 in combat with Spitfires). *(PK)*

Above: 2.(F)/123 flew intensively in the Eastern Mediterranean area. Crews celebrated the 1000th combat mission on 14 December 1941; the 2000th on 23 August 1942 and the 3000th on 14 April 1943. Shown here is the ceremony for the 4000th mission, led by Lt. Hessinger's crew on 23 September 1943. The scene is at Tatoi (one of Athens' airfields). Notice the pennant with the unit's crest. The returning crew (Lt. Hessinger, Ofw. Dörries, Ofw. Huster and Uffz. Fastenrot) stands in front of the Ju 88. Not surprisingly, Helmut Dörries and Franz Hessinger received the Knight's Cross in August 1944. Fastenrot was later killed near Derna in 1944. Units such as this suffered heavy casualties, for instance 2.(F)/123 flew more than 200 operations in a single month; which helps to explain loss rates of up to 600% for some recce units.
(*Eppler*)

Below left: In the last quarter of 1943, General der Luftwaffe Martin Fiebig came to Crete to review Luftwaffe units who faced the growing threat of an invasion in the Balkans. His He 111 was escorted from Heraklion to Athens by Bf 109G-6s of 7./JG 27. A *Kriegsberichter* (war reporter) accompanying the General took this picture of the escort and later gave a copy of it to the pilots.
(*Alfred Heckmann*)

Below right: In the first months of 1944, the vital oilfields of Ploesti (Romania) were defended by a few German fighters alongside the Royal Rumanian Air Force. But the American bombers of XVth Air Force coming from Southern Italy had to fly over the Balkans. To cover this area, II./JG 51 was dispatched to Yugoslavia (mainly to Nisch) and operated not only against bombers flying to Romania but also against those flying to Austria (and the valuable aircraft factories at Wiener-Neustadt) via the Ljubjana gap. Shown here is Bf 109G-6 'White 7' (WNr.163269) of Ofw. Elias-Paul Kühlein of 4./JG 51. It was photographed on the Bulgarian airfield of Radomir; as Nisch was repeatedly the target of American formations, II./JG 51 often had to evacuate to more secure locations. Notice the eye painted on the cowling 'bump' covering the MG 131, a design used only by this unit.
(*Elias-Paul Kühlein*)

Above and right: **Around September 1943, KG 54 adopted this 'mottle' camouflage. Ju 88 'B3 + AL' of 3./KG 54 is seen flying over the Alps, perhaps on a ferry flight from Munich to Italy. The *Totenkopf* Geschwader operated in Italy all through 1943 before being called home to the Reich in December of that year. In the second photo, the four-man crew of Lt. Peter Schulz are photographed in front of their Ju 88 of I./KG 54. The new camouflage is clearly visible but the death's head, the unit's crest, seems not to be painted on the nose. In 1944, Schulz was transferred to I./KG 66 (the German 'pathfinder' unit), although this time his Ju 88s had a crew of only three. He was shot down on 23 January 1945 near Aalst (Belgium) but survived to become a POW.**
(Remy Chuinard and Peter Schulz)

Above left: In February 1944, III./JG 77 was recalled to Germany to fly in the *Reichsverteidigung* (Home Defence). The sole unit left in Greece to cover the Aegean area was 7./JG 77, although it was given some additional aircraft. This Staffel was distributed in *Schwärme* on Greek airfields on Crete, Rhodes and the mainland. Bf 109G-5 'White 3' of the Austrian Uffz. Franz Stadler is seen here on the Cretan airfield of Kastelli, fitted with an additional fuel tank to increase its range against British raiders engaged in shipping attacks. At the end of May 1944, 7./JG 77 returned to Austria, leaving the area to 6./JG 51.
(Franz Stadler)

Above right: On 9 May 1944, the Cretan village of Samonas was forcibly evacuated as a reprisal for partisan attacks. The Luftwaffe was ordered to destroy the village, but at the time had very few aircraft available. So Ar 196 floatplanes of Seeaufklärungsgruppe 126 were used to drop bombs on the houses. This photo is thus very unusual: seaplanes flying over mountainous country playing at *Stukas*. Note the unit code (a small 'D1') and the white band around the fuselage.
(Kroll)

Left: In 1944, German reconnaissance units in the Mediterranean could no longer operate Hs 126s in the face of Allied air power. 1./NAG 12 was one such unit with a long history. It operated in Poland, France and the USSR before being disbanded. A new 1.(H)/12 was raised in the summer of 1942 from the remnants of other units. In 1943, 1.(H)/12 received Bf 109G-6s and moved in October to Albania (after the collapse of the Italian army). Based at Tirana and Devoli (Berat), the unit flew recce missions along the Albanian coast, and also over the Italian mainland (Bari/Brindisi). Losses were heavy. An Allied interrogation report from May 1944 stated that the entire strength had been twice replaced since October 1943! This photo shows a celebration held at Berat for a special combat mission. Note the additional tank for long range operations over the Adriatic. Note too the insignia on the top of the wreath. The crest, rarely painted on the aircraft, was the insignia of the disbanded I./Aufkl.Gr. 10 *Tannenberg* whose components had been included in the unit.
(Troebs Family)

Above and below: The main supply route in the Balkans was the sole railway line going from Klagenfurt to Athens via Zagreb, Belgrade and Salonika. It was often cut by partisans and had to be supplemented by air transport. In 1944, the Ju 52s of TG 4 were used to supply the German garrisons in Greece, Albania and Yugoslavia. The first photo shows a three-engined machine from the unit taking off from a dusty Balkan airfield. Note the white underwing tips. The second shows another *Tante Ju* of the same Gruppe flying over mountainous Balkan country. Some Ju 52s were destroyed in Greece/Crete, victims of intruders coming from Egypt; others were shot down over the Albanian or Yugoslavian coasts, being easy prey for attackers from Italy.
(J-L. Roba)

CHAPTER SIXTEEN

In the West, 1943–1944

Secret report of attack on convoy by German composite aircraft:

On 24 June 1944, an attack upon an Allied convoy is reported to have been made by a German composite aircraft. The incident was witnessed by the pilot and navigator of a Mosquito.

(1) The Mosquito was on patrol 25 miles west of Le Havre at 23.00hr at an altitude of 5000 to 6000 feet. Visibility was excellent...

(2) Both occupants had a good view, lasting for 15 to 20 seconds, of an unusual biplane about a mile away. This had the appearance of a small aircraft attached to the top of a larger twin-engined type . . .

(3) Although the Mosquito was flown on a parallel course and must have been seen, no avoiding action was taken by the composite which proceeded on a dead straight course in the direction of the convoy . . .

(4) Whilst the crew of the Mosquito were striving to identify the composite, the smaller aircraft lifted suddenly from the lower component, banked steeply, flew away at right angles, and was lost against the land background. The larger aircraft then turned over on its back and dived straight into the sea without showing any tendency to glide. It reached the sea in about 3 seconds . . . On striking the water, it caused a terrific explosion and orange flash, three miles east of the convoy . . .

(PRO archives AIR 40/186, the first report of an attack launched by a Mistel composite, probably of IV./KG 101)

Above and below: **On 30 January 1943, Fw. Kromer of 5./JG 1 belly-landed his FW 190A-4 'Black 10' (WNr. 7032) near Woensdrecht airfield. The pilot was unhurt but his aircraft was classed as 45 per cent destroyed. At this time, II./JG 1 was the first line of defence against Allied raids, especially the large formations of four-engined 'heavies'. It was usually the first unit to intercept the raids heading for north Germany. In the summer of 1943 the Gruppe was sent back to the Rhine. Notice the red *Tatzelwurm* Staffel badge on the cowling.**

Right: In the spring of 1943, the Germans realised that the Luftwaffe's traditional tactics were unable to prevent increasingly heavy bombing raids on the towns and industries of the Fatherland. Fighter units tested a range of new tactics and weapons with varying results. On 22 March 1943, Lt. Heinz Knoke (of 2./JG 1) tried a new idea by dropping a time-fused bomb into the middle of a Flying Fortress 'box'. He brought down one bomber. Following that success, other fighter units tried to do the same. This picture shows a FW 190A-4 of I./JG 1 (ex-IV./JG 1) loaded with such a bomb. Notice the antenna under the port wing for the FuG 16Z-E radio, normally used for commanders' aircraft.

Left: General Adolf Galland visited 8./JG 1 at Leeuwarden in early 1943 with his personal aircraft, a Siebel Si 104. Notice the different emblems on the fuselage: the eagle's head (JG 51 *Mölders*), the wolf's head (Ergänzungszerstörergruppe), the winged 'U' (JG 3 *Udet*) and the sword (JG 52).

Right: In January and February 1943, JG 26 received its first FW190 A-5s. Here a pilot of I./JG 26 describes his latest combat to his comrades by waving his hands in the time-honoured way. Note the yellow wing tips and panel under the cowling, and the light paint of the A-5 in the background.

Left: At the beginning of 1943, KG 40 was deployed around Western Europe. When I./KG 40 was reformed at Fassberg (equipped with He 177s), III./KG 40 (with FW 200s) and V./KG 40 (with Ju 88s) operated against shipping, under the command of Fliegerführer Atlantik. At that time, the II./KG 40 was based at the Dutch airfield of Soesterberg, acting as a school unit. Shown here is Do 217E-2/4 'F8 + CP' belonging to the 6th Staffel. The entire Gruppe flew this type. In June 1943, II./KG 40 was renamed V./KG 2, while a new II./KG 40 (with He 177s) was created in September 1943.

Above, left and right: To counter the German submarine menace in the Atlantic, RAF Coastal Command tried to attack the *U-Booten* leaving their bases or returning from a mission, when they were at their most vulnerable. To protect them, the Luftwaffe created a special unit of heavy fighters, V./KG 40, operating near U-boat bases or over the Bay of Biscay to intercept the British raiders. In 1943, V./KG 40 was renamed I./ZG 1 and flew mainly from bases in Brittany (Vannes and Lorient). The first photo shows a Ju 88 of the unit circling over a submarine returning to Lorient. The second shows a I./ZG 1 crew returning from a mission, all wearing kapok life vests. Note the guns in the solid nose of the Ju 88C-6. **(PK)**

Right: Another new anti-bomber weapon tested in JG 1 was the 21cm rocket launcher *Do Werfer* ('stove pipe'). It was successful at first, but Allied escort fighters soon learned to look out for the heavily laden rocket-carrying machines. They were easy prey for the Mustangs and Thunderbolts.

Left: In April 1943, in the face of ever-increasing intrusions of Allied bombers into its area of operation (the Low Countries and the German Bight), JG 1 had to be reinforced. On 1 April 1943, the Geschwader gave birth to JG 11, providing two Gruppen for the new unit (I. and III./JG 1). JG 1 then had to rebuild one Gruppe (III./JG 1) and rename the existing IV./JG 1 as I./JG 1). Several experienced pilots formed the core of the new III./JG 1, including Lt. Eugen Wintergerst (Stk. of 9./JG 1). He is seen here after having made the new Gruppe's first kill, on 11 June 1943.

Right: After the losses in Africa and over Stalingrad, German transport units suffered from a lack of machines at the beginning of 1943. But the Luftwaffe had access to the remnants of the French aircraft industries as the Wehrmacht had overrun Vichy Southern France in November 1942. Not only did they find aircraft such as the LèO 451 bomber, but they also captured the Liorè et Olivier plants at Marignane and Ambèrieu. The bombers were quickly transformed into LèO 451T transports and used mainly in TG 4 in the West. In September 1943, after Italy's surrender, more Italian machines were also included in the transport order of battle.
(Jean-Pierre Chantrain)

Above: The newly created JG 11 was posted to the northern flank of its sister-squadron (JG 1) and was tasked with defending the German Bight, from Northern Germany to Denmark. These FW 190As of 3./JG 11 are in readiness (with starter power trolleys plugged in) at Husum in late summer 1943. Note the Staffel insignia on the engine-cowling, as well as a white band after the *Balkenkreuz*. A red diagonal band alongside the cockpit is visible on the most distant machine, an unusual marking used by leaders in JG 11 at this time.

Above: In spring 1943, black/white, black/red or black/yellow checkerboard patterns were painted on the cowlings of aircraft belonging to the 1st, 2nd and 3rd Staffels of I./JG 1. This FW 190A-4 is unusual in that it wears black/white squares with a 'Yellow 6' marking (the squares indicating that the aircraft belongs to the 1st Staffel, and the number colour, to the 3rd). This machine was probably transferred from one Staffel to the other just before it crashed.

Above: After several months in the USSR, II./JG 3 was posted to Schiphol in September 1943 to form an outpost for the defence of Germany. It was given the dangerous task of being the first to intercept the large Allied bomber formations passing over the Netherlands to the Reich. The Gruppe was led by a renowned ace: Major Kurt Brändle. His Bf 109G-6, fitted with an Erla canopy, wears the double Chevron. The Kommandeur was killed in action on 3 November 1943 after shooting down two P-47 Thunderbolts. His final tally stood at 180 victories (including 25 in the West).

Above left: On 5 November 1943, the VIIIth US Air Force attacked Münster and Gelsenkirchen marshalling yards. 503 bombers escorted by 383 fighters took part, and the escort fighters claimed 19 victories, 5 of them by the 353 FG. Here, Lt. Leroy Ista of 352 FS/353 FG gives the *coup de grâce* to a *Gustav* (his sole victory) near Gelsenkirchen. His victim is probably Uffz. Robert Pautner's Bf 109G-6 (WNr.15408) 'White 12' of 9./JG 26. The pilot baled out but was severely wounded.

Above right: Transferred from 11./JG 51 (through several days at JG 2) to III./JG 1 (where he took command of the 7th Staffel), Oblt. Heinz Klöpper continued to increase his tally despite the stronger opposition in the west than the east. On 13 November 1943, he had to make an emergency landing with his Bf 109G-6 'White 1' after having been hit in combat. On 29 November, he was not so lucky. While entering a dogfight over the Netherlands, he dived and crashed along with both wingmen, having misread his altitude. He was credited with 94 victories (including 13 in the west and 8 four-engined).

Right: At the end of December 1943, JG 1 and JG 11 received their first FW 190A-7s. These were different from earlier versions mainly in their armament. The 7.92mm MG 17s over the engine cowling had gone, but were replaced by heavier 13mm MG 131s. Here, a FW 190A-7 of JG 11 is photographed in early 1944 on Aalborg-Ost airfield.

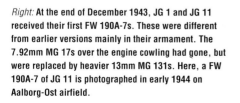

Left: **Photographed in 1944 at Venlo (Netherlands), a rare Ju 88R-2 of the *Nachtjagd* (Nightfighter Force) has camouflage paint obliterating all the markings. It is the aircraft of Lt. Erich Jung of II./NJG 2 who claimed a number of victories in the west against the RAF's attack on the railways (the so-called Transportation Plan) preceding the invasion in Normandy. Note the SN-2 radar (nicknamed *Hertegewei*) and the armament (four cannon) in the nose.**
(Erich Jung)

Right and below: **From mid-1943, KG 6 was based on Belgian airfields (Chièvres and Melsbroek). In the second half of the year, the Gruppe was sent to intervene in Italy and Greece. At the beginning of 1944, I./KG 6 came back to Chièvres (it moved in April to Brétigny, France) while III./KG 6 was again in Melsbroek. The unit operated in the new *Blitz* over England (the famous *Unternehmen Steinbock*). Here, a Ju 188 of I Gruppe is photographed at Chièvres. Note the wavy camouflage pattern adopted for night operations.**
(Hermann Hogeback)

124

Right: **GIs examine the remnants of Ju 88 'B3 + H?' of KG 54 *Totenkopf* shot down over the Normandy beachhead. The bomber still wears the unusual camouflage adopted a year earlier in Italy. I. and III./KG 54 launched their first attacks on the evening of 6 June 1944, flying from Juvincourt (France) and Soesterberg (Netherlands). Their last operation in that campaign was during the night of 28/29 August 1944 against bridges over the Seine near Melun.**
(USAAF via Van Mol)

Left: **On 6 June 1944 at 08.30hr, Stab III./JG 3 was put at readiness. The official notification that the invasion had begun arrived 13 minutes later. Ten hours later, 45 Bf 109G-6s deployed to St Andrè (60 miles/100 km west of Paris), from where the pilots flew a hard Normandy campaign from June to August 1944. This Bf 109 *Gustav* 'Yellow (Red?) 6' of III./JG 3 made a belly-landing at Pullay (near Verneuil sur Eure). Its decorations are contradictory: the insignia on the engine cowling is the winged 'U' of JG 3 *Udet*, but the Defence of the Reich band after the *Balkenkreuz* seems to be yellow (or red) . . . and JG 3 wore a white one. Note also the vertical bar in this band, the marking of a IIIrd Gruppe.**

Right: **Western France, summer 1944. Photographed while mechanics were refilling its tanks, a FW 190A-8 of 5./JG 1 is hidden in the trees near its landing strip. Note the wide spiral on the spinner.**

Left and below: **German airfields in occupied countries often had false airfields constructed nearby. The decoy was usually a field with a few mocked-up buildings and dummy aircraft. This became vital in Normandy, when airfields were continually being surveyed and were under the constant threat of attack. The first photo shows a false Bf 109 liberated in August 1944 on a field in Normandy. The practice was not reserved for the frontline, as the second photo of a fake Ju 88 (photographed at Aalborg at the end of the war) shows.**

Left: **When Allied troops liberated Brussels in September 1944, they found some abandoned derelict aircraft, such as this elderly Do 17E (or F?) on Melsbroeck airfield. 'GS + NE' was possibly a plane of a Luftdienstkommando or a hack for the unit based on the airfield.**
(J-L. Roba)

Above, left and right: **In the Normandy Campaign, the Luftwaffe suffered many losses against Allied aerial superiority. Many aircraft were shot down in combat, such as 'Black 5' shown in the first photo (presumed to be Ogfr. Max Ulrich Förster's FW 190 of 2./JG 1, reported MIA on 28 July 1944 in the St Lö area). Others were captured on airfields overrun by the advancing troops (such as this FW 190 of an unknown III Gruppe examined at Nogent-le-Roi in mid-August 1944).**
(US National Archives)

Below: **The Heinkel 177 *Greif* (Griffon) was an ambitious project which never lived up to its potential. It was a four-engined bomber, with two paired engines in each nacelle driving the two propellers. This unusual configuration was unreliable, and the *Greif* was prone to engine fires. Two prototypes were evaluated by IV./KG 40 in Bordeaux-Mèrignac. Here it was wanted by the Kriegsmarine to protect the U-boat force by attacking long-range fighters and convoy escorts. One planned use was as a *Fernzerstörer* (long-range 'destroyer'), the other as a *Torpedoflugzeug* (torpedo bomber). The He 177 also flew with I./KG 50 in the Stalingrad aerial bridge (at the beginning of 1943) as a transport plane. In October 1943, I./KG 50 became II./KG 40 and the unit flew under control of the Fliegeführer Atlantik. KG 40 and KG 100 also employed the He 177 in Operation *Steinbock*, the renewed *Blitz* on England. This He 177 was found by advancing Allied units in 1944 on Chateaudun airfield and was probably from 1./KG 40 as this Gruppe was also equipped with the *Greif*. Note the large, solid landing gear.**
(US National Archives)

CHAPTER SEVENTEEN

Norway, 1943–1945

On 25 April 1943, I came back from a night bombing mission on Murmansk which occurred between 1.05 and 2.35hr. I went to sleep immediately because, in spite of my very short night, I was on duty the following morning. My comrade, Lt. Gerhard Schwab, and I went to meet the technical Officer, Oblt. Maul who told us that the unit had only four serviceable aircraft. So I had to pilot again my old Bf 110 Dora 'IB + AX' ('Anton'), the aircraft used the night before. That twin-engined machine was well known in the Staffel for continual technical troubles. But I myself never had a problem.

That day, our mission was a normal one over the sea to protect a maritime convoy. I took off alongside Schwab in his Bf 110 at 10.51hr and headed towards the sea. When we reached our first destination, we began to circle at a height of 600 metres. We were called by radio and warned that enemies were approaching from behind. We looked and finally saw two twin-engined aircraft, identified first as Bf 110s. We thought that they came to replace us. But they were then four and their number grew to eight. This was quite strange because including our two aircraft, our unit had only four machines serviceable at Kirkenes. I finally understood that I had misidentified the types: Soviet Pe-2s were easily confused with the Bf 110 as they too had twin engines and a double fin! I could see the red star.

We were flying at a higher altitude than the Soviets and Schwab dived onto them. He was very impatient for his first victory, having been posted to JG 5 for more than one year. I was in the unit for about four weeks and it was my first aerial battle. I dived too and attacked at a fantastic speed, firing without stop. Pushed by my dive and my speed, I flew along the formation of Pe 2s, a very dangerous position as all the Soviet rear gunners could concentrate their fire on my aircraft. Nevertheless, it was possible that I had killed or wounded one or two gunners. The fight became very confused and I saw then with horror that I had already spent all my ammunition in that exciting dive. But I was lucky because my aircraft was an old 'D' which could be reloaded from inside (which was impossible in

the more recent types). My radio/observer, Uffz. Walter Bengard was able to load a new ammunition cartridge in the machine gun. It was just in time because a Pe-2 appeared suddenly in front of me and I could fire on him, destroying both engines. It then crashed into the sea. I saw a second smoke column and thought that Schwab had passed over his misfortune by claiming his first victory. I was right, and very happy by this surprise fight, we landed at Kirkenes at 12.45hr.

(Lt. Wolfgang Wollenweber, 13.(Z)/JG 5)

Above and left: **Hauptmann Heinrich Ehrler is probably the best-known ace of JG 5. He arrived in Norway in February 1941 when his unit was still I./JG 77. His Gruppe was renamed II./JG 5 in January 1942 and from that moment, his tally (opened in autumn 1941) continually increased. In September 1942, he received the *Ritterkreuz* after some 64 claims. The first photo was probably taken in January 1943 when the rudder of his 'Yellow 12' showed 70 victories. He claimed his 100th on 5 June 1943 and received the *Eichenlaub* (Oak Leaves) on 2 August 1943 for his 112th claim. The second picture (showing 115 *Abschüsse*) was taken shortly after.**

128

Above left: **In February 1943, Hptm. Friedrich-Wilhelm Strakeljahn formed 14.(Jabo)/JG 5. The unit became very active along the Norwegian coast and claimed many successes against Allied shipping. In the beginning, the 14th Staffel was equipped with FW 190A-2s and A-3s, already obsolescent at that time. Here, in summer 1943, mechanics are attaching a bomb to the centreline pylon (used for bombs or the auxiliary tank) of one of the Staffel's aircraft.**

Right: **In order to maintain contact with the German garrisons in the *Hohe Nord* (the 'far north'), the Luftwaffe used Ju 52 floatplanes. They could land in fjords, bringing supplies and evacuating wounded and sick soldiers. The picture shows the crew of such a Ju 52 (*See*) float plane being brought by boat to their frozen machine to prepare for a mission. They will first have to clear the snow and ice from it and free up all moving control surfaces.**
(PK)

Left: **In the winter of 1943–44, some Bf 109G-6s of I./JG 5 were fitted with cannon in underwing gondolas. With the supplementary armament, this aircraft had impressive firepower: two MG 131 13mm heavy machine-guns above the engine, a 20mm MG 151 firing through the propeller, and two MG 151s in the gondolas. Here, Lt. Heinrich von Podewils stands in front of his *Gustav*.**

Above: In July 1944, the *Zerstörerstaffel* of JG 5 was detached from the Geschwader and renamed 10./ZG 26. Posted to Trondheim-Lade in December, it went back to JG 5 in February 1945, as part of its II Gruppe, under command of Hptm. Herbert Treppe. This photo was taken at this time, showing combat . . . with snowballs, in front of a Bf 110G-2.

Above: Herdla, spring 1945. This close-up of FW 190A-8 'Blue 9' of 12./JG 5 shows details of the canopy. Note the cable of the *Anlasswagen* (power trolley) plugged in, as well as the Revi gunsight.

Below: Winter 1943/44. Operating over wild empty countryside and out to sea, it was necessary to have long-range aircraft capable of searching for downed flyers. This FW 58 *Weihe* of II./JG 5 flew many such missions and its crewmen took part in the rescue of several pilots.

Above: Compared with their comrades fighting desperately on other fronts, the JG 5 pilots who operated in northern Europe had a quieter war's end. Photographed in the spring of 1945 at Herdla, this FW 190A-8 is fitted with an auxiliary 300 litre tank and is flown by Uffz. Gerhard Eisermann of IV./JG 5.

Above: The western coast of Norway in 1944/1945. This Do 24 (perhaps belonging to 5. Seenotstaffel) rescued several pilots shot down over the Eismeer. Oblt. Werner Gayko (Stk of 5./JG 5) was saved by this aircraft in the spring of 1945.

Below: On 5 April 1945, Oblt. Karl-Heinz Koch (Staffelkapitän of 13./JG 5) crash-landed near Herdla (Norway) with his FW 190A-8 'Blue 9'. Classified as 70 per cent destroyed, this was one of the last combat losses of IV./JG 5.

CHAPTER EIGHTEEN

Defence of the Reich

On 4 January 1944, I scrambled with the Gruppe at 10.05hr as a Rottenführer (leader of a two plane group) of 4./JG 1. At 10.20hr, at 4000 metres height, we saw at 7000 metres, SW of Münster, two boxes of around 40 Flying Fortresses, each with a good fighter escort. I climbed to a Boeing left 500 metres behind the others. Despite the fact that Thunderbolts were hanging 100 metres over it, I could make two attacks from the rear flying as near as possible. One of its starboard engines was destroyed and a part of the fuselage and the fin exploded. The Boeing lost a lot of height. As I launched my third attack (from the side), I myself became the target of the Thunderbolts. My plane was nearly ripped apart, being so many times hit on the wings and the fin that I had to break off my attack and try to land as soon as possible. My Rottenflieger (wingman), Ofw. Liper, saw a last time at 2000 meters the B-17 I had attacked. It crashed at 12.00hr in square JN 5/5 (Zeddam/ 10 km N. of Emmerich).

[Following that report, Fuchs's FW 190A-6 'White 2' (WNr. 470077) fired 300 rounds with its MG 17s and 368 more with its MG 151/20s. One American crewman was killed and another became POW. The eight survivors may have been helped to escape by the Dutch underground movements. Fw. Heinz Fuchs was KIA on 24 February 1944, south of Minden, victim of the defensive fire of a B-24. He was credited with 11 victories.]

Combat report of Fw. Heinz Fuchs of 4./JG 1

Above: **A very rare bird! Photographed apparently on an airfield near Munich (one can read *Wetterflugdienst München*), this FW A-47 'VB + QH' is one of the twenty such machines fitted with special equipment for meteorological purposes. (*J-L. Roba*)**

Right: **On 25 December 1943, II./JG 3 left the Netherlands to return to Rotenburg (near Bremen) to be more centrally placed for the defence of the Reich. After several weeks' rest, the Gruppe went back to action in February 1944. Lt. Karl-Heinz Koch (centre, in front of a Bf 109G-6) took command of 4. Staffel after the death in combat (on 24 October 1943) of his Kapitän and ace, Hptm. Werner Lucas. Notice the winged 'U', insignia of JG 3 *Udet*.**

Right and below: **Zerstörergeschwader ZG 76 actually had two careers. The first unit to bear the name was disbanded at the end of 1940, its components spread around various other units. The second ZG 76 was raised at the end of 1943 to oppose the American day bomber formations which were pounding German cities. In May 1944, the entire Geschwader changed its Bf 110s to Me 410s (such as these examples from II Gruppe), but the new fighter was no match for the large Allied fighter escorts. Losses were heavy and, in July 1944, I./ZG 76 trained on Bf 109s to become I./JG 76. II./ZG 76 received FW 190s to become IV./JG 54.**
(Karl-Fritz Schloßstein)

Right: **Dortmund at the beginning of 1944. At this time the Stab I./JG 1 FW 190A-6s were adorned with black and white bands around the engine cowlings for recognition purposes. This aircraft belongs to the Kommandeur, Major Emil Schnoor (although the undersurface does not carry the bands). First named IV./JG 1, this Gruppe was redesignated I./JG 1 in April 1943.**

Above left and right: **In 1944, Me 410s of the** *Zerstörergruppen* **were fitted with the fearsome 5 cm BK Automatic Aircraft Gun. While the gun allowed the** *Zerstörer* **to inflict great damage on a bomber from a distance, it further diminished its manoeuvrability against the Allied fighter escort. In the summer of 1944, most of the** *Zerstörergruppen* **of the** *Reichsverteidigung* **were disbanded and their pilots quickly retrained for single-engined fighters. The first photo shows Me 410s of II./ZG 76 at Königsberg/Neumarkt. Both pictures show how the gun barrel extended by at least 3 feet (1m) beyond the nose of the aircraft.**

Below: **Uffz. Fritz Buchholz in his Me 410 of II./ZG 76. He is wearing a steel helmet, an unusual practice for Luftwaffe flyers. With the rest of his comrades, Buchholz was transferred to single-engined fighters in II./JG 6 in the summer of 1944. Notice the rear firing gun in the barbette near the tiny fuselage code '3U'.**

Above: **In most histories of air warfare, the role of the ferry units of any air force is usually ignored. In the Luftwaffe as well as the RAF, men (and women too) flew new machines to the front units, an important task without glory but still dangerous. Many ferry pilots were killed in bad weather or shot down by intruders, while accidents also took their toll.**

Lt. Wolfgang Betz joined 2./JG 77 in Italy in July 1943. On 12 November 1943, he was wounded in a flying incident. After recovering, he was no longer fit for front-line service and was transferred to *Überführungsgeschwader 1,* **a ferry unit. On 10 July 1944, he had to crash-land a Bf 109 near Frankfurt am Oder, and his aircraft (wearing** *Stammkennzeichen* **'?? + XB') was destroyed. Injured a second time, Betz didn't fly again before the end of the war.**
(Wolfgang Betz)

Above and right: A special assault Staffel (Sturmstaffel 1) was created at the end of 1943, manned by pilots who volunteered to shoot down at least one four-engined bomber on every mission, even if they had to ram it. To allow pilots to get close enough to the heavily defended bombers, their FW 190s were fitted with extra armour plating around the cockpit area. The results gained by Sturmstaffel 1 were not spectacular, but were enough to spur the formation of three such fighter Gruppen: IV.(Sturm)/JG 3, II.(Sturm)/JG 4 and II.(Sturm)/JG 300. FW 190A-8s of the latter unit were photographed at Holzkirchen at the beginning of August 1944. Clearly visible are the thick armour plates under the cockpit.

Left: **Alfred Nitsch (born in 1920 in Austria) joined the Luftwaffe in 1941. He trained in A/B Schule 61 (Oschatz) and was so good a pilot that he remained there as instructor. In 1944, he volunteered for the front and, after retraining, was sent to 9./JG 77 in September 1944. He is seen here at Neuruppen in his brand-new Bf 109K-4 which had just equipped III./JG 77. Notice the unit's crest on the nose of the fighter and the yellow armband on the pilot's left arm. Marked** *Deutsche Luftwaffe* **with an eagle and swastika, it was worn to prevent a downed pilot being lynched by an angry mob believing that he was an allied airmen, a** *Luftgangster* **of German propaganda. Nitsch survived the war and died in 1995.**
(Alfred Nitsch)

Right: After having suffered heavy losses in Normandy, I./JG 1 was called back to Germany for several weeks to rest and regroup. In November 1944, the Gruppe went into action again in defence of the Reich from its Greifswald airfield. The action was fierce, and the losses in November and December 1944 were horrific. The red band of *Reichsverteidigung* is clearly shown on this FW 190A-8 of 2./JG 1.

135

Left: On 17 December 1944, I./JG 1 left Greifswald (from where it had been defending Berlin) and once more moved west, up to the front line. The Gruppe was brought forward to support the Wehrmacht's last offensive in the West, known later as the Battle of the Bulge. Lt. Gerhard Stiemer (3./JG 1) was ferrying this FW 190A-8 'Yellow 8' when he suffered engine trouble and had to make a belly-landing near Celle. The aircraft was slightly damaged. Note the red *Reichsverteidigung* band behind the outline *Balkenkreuz*. A red band indicated that the aircraft belonged to JG 1 or JG 300.

Right: At the end of November 1944, II./JG 26 received their first FW 190D-9s. In contrast to the earlier radial-engined FW 190s, the *Dora* had a 12-cylinder in-line power plant, which caused the nose to be lengthened. The new engine gave the FW 190 a spectacular increase in performance, making it at least the equal of any Allied fighter, and superior to many. Oblt. Adolf Glunz, who signed this photo, was an ace of II./JG 26 and ended the war with 72 victories (including 69 in the West).

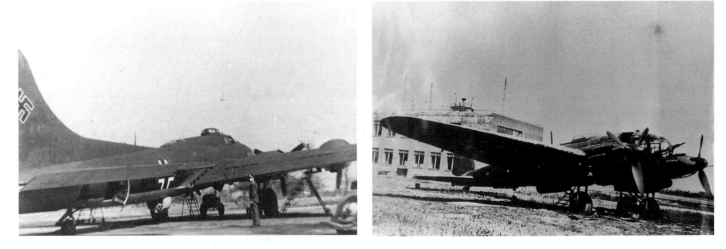

Above, left and right: Much has been written about KG 200 and its secret special missions. Renowned for making use of captured enemy aircraft (such as this B-17), it also operated with more conventional machines, such as this blackened He 111H photographed at Prague/Ruzyn. Barely visible is the tiny white-painted 'A3' code of the Geschwader.

CHAPTER NINETEEN

The Last Months in the East

I had been appointed Kommodore of JG 51 on 1 April 1944. Exactly one year later, I was ordered to leave my Geschwaderstab to take immediate command of JG 77. It was so sudden that I could not officially transfer the command to my successor. So I started alone from Garz/ Rügen to Märisch/Ostrau (Czechoslovakia), the location of my new Geschwaderstab. I was stressed all along the journey: I had no chance to escape if I was intercepted alone by a Soviet Squadron, but I landed without problem. After several heavy combats over Brünn (Brno) and Southern Czechoslovakia, I received the order from Feldmarschall Schörner to build a special unit with the goal of securing the withdrawal of Wehrmacht units to the west. This unit had to be raised at Königgrätz with one fighter squadron of JG 77, one recce and one ground attack Staffel. I remained some days with my JG 77 Staffel in our new base, waiting for orders and for the other planned Staffeln that never joined us. I was forbidden to use the radio, we could only receive orders and not send anything. On 8 May, some Czechs came to us, giving us news of the German surrender and asking for our weapons. Without any orders, I did not accept this and ordered them to go away. I knew that they would soon come back and try to capture our base by force. It was very hard to resist, our situation was very dangerous and, faced with the lack of news, I called all my men together during the afternoon. I told the pilots that they had to fly towards the West as far as possible and, if they could, directly to their native towns. I then turned to the ground personnel and began to organize their evacuation. A He 111 landed a few hours later and could load all the Luftwaffe female auxiliaries. The crew members confirmed to me that Germany had capitulated on 8 May. All the remaining personnel (incl. pilots whose aircraft were out of order) then climbed into a Ju 52. I flew it and took off with some fear: we were 46 of us, hoping to land in Deggendorf. Over Plattling, we were hit by light American AA which forced me to land. For us, the war ended in a lucky manner, we had avoided Soviet captivity.

(Major Fritz Losigkeit, Kommodore of JG 77)

Above: **Unteroffizier Anton Tonschi Hacker was born in 1921 in Marienbad in the Sudeten. After his training, he joined 8./JG 77 at the end of 1943 and was sent to Romania. The young pilot is seen here on Mizil airfield, probably around March 1944. Notice the red heart, the unit's crest (derived from the insignia of the late Kommodore Müncheberg when he led 7./JG 26) and, under the wing, one of the two *Werferrohren* for 21cm rockets (fitted at the beginning of 1944). Tonschi Hacker will claim an American Liberator in April but will himself be shot down and killed on 5 April 1944.** *(Karl-Heinz Büttner)*

Above: **Same time, same place. Leutnant Martin Ludwig sits on his Bf 109G-2 'Black 9' (WNr.14107), also of 8./JG 77, the only squadron of JG 77 fitted with the 21cm rocket launchers.**

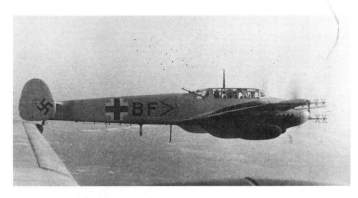

Above left: In mid-1943, the Luftwaffe raised a new nightfighter Gruppe, IV./NJG 6, after night attacks by the Soviet Air Force on the Romanian oilfields of Ploesti. The high-ranking officers (Kommandeur and Staffelkapitäne) were all veterans of other units. IV./NJG 6 had only two German squadrons (the 10th and 11th). 12./NJG 6 was constituted with Romanian personnel hastily trained for that purpose. Nightfighters in that theatre were painted in bright colours (RLM 76 with light patches of RLM 75). Here, in the first months of 1944, '2Z + BF' (of Stab IV./NJG 6) is seen flying near Russe (on the Romanian/Bulgarian border).
(Hans Meyer)

Above right: At the end of 1943, 17 Army was encircled by the Russians in the Crimea. The troops had to be supplied and evacuated by air, and an aerial bridge was operated until 11 May 1944, the official date of the end of evacuation operations. Transportfliegerführer 2 assembled some units as I./TG 5 (equipped with Me 323s). This machine 'C8 + F?' was photographed on the Romanian airfield of Zilistea, the Gruppe's base. The aircraft carries the narrow yellow fuselage band of the Eastern Front. In May, the six-engined aircraft will return to Germany before being recalled again to Romania in August 1944 to help with the German evacuation of the country.
(Martin Bauer)

Left and above: To counter the menace of magnetic mines dropped by RAF bombers in German-held waters, the Luftwaffe raised a special unit, Minensuchgruppe 1 from a nucleus called *Sonderkommando Mausi*. It was equipped with the Ju 52 *Mausi*, a special variant fitted with a large magnetic ring. The three-engined transport would fly low and slow over the water, in the hope that the magnetic field would detonate any mines present. The task was dangerous, and some aircraft were destroyed by mine blast as they flew just a little too low. The first photo shows *Mausi* 'NJ(?) + NF' with the ring under the fuselage. This Ju 52 was probably photographed in the Southern theatre (note the white band). The close-up above (taken in Crete) shows the insignia of *Sonderkdo. Mausi*.
(Peter Taghon and J-Ch. Verrycken)

Right: The sole Do 24 unit operating in the Black Sea was 8. Seenotstaffel. So, in April 1944, when the troops in the Crimea were cut off, an additional temporary unit was formed from aircraft donated by the other sea rescue squadrons. *Sonderstaffel Mamaia* was based in that Romanian city and comprised aircraft supplied by at least five Seenot units. This machine (perhaps belonging to 5 Seenot) is seen here being loaded at Sebastopol harbour.

Left: As did many other fighter units, JG 11 left the Western Front in January 1945 to shore up the collapsing Eastern Front. Skilled at operating against Western Allied air superiority, the JG 11 pilots were able to claim significant numbers of victories in the East, for only a few losses. They then followed the general westwards retreat and were finally posted near Berlin in order to protect the city. This photo was taken in Strausberg (near the city) in March 1945. Four pilots wearing full-leather dress are standing with a Bf 109G-14/AS.

Right: From the beginning of 1945, the Luftwaffe was forced to throw more and more pilots into action with inadequate training. Each training unit had an *Einstaz* (combat) Staffel, but the trainees were often involved in fighting even when they didn't belong to this squadron. This was the case for most pilots of EJG 1, based in the Berlin area. Here, one of their FW 190A-8s is being repaired, after the landing gear mechanism was damaged in combat.

CHAPTER TWENTY

Final Months in the West

At the end of 1944, I came back to I./JG 1 that I had left after the fighting over the invasion front. Now, everything had changed. Most of my comrades had disappeared; some had been posted to other units, but the great majority had been killed in action. I could feel the changed mood. The fact that we, the officers, were quartered separately from the soldiers had become familiar since our departure from Schiphol, and certainly did not reinforce the link between the men in the Staffel; but now a deep fracture appeared in the Officers' Corps itself. The attitudes adopted by each of us (so close to death) were radically different. And I think that this behaviour was created by the belonging of individuals to different social classes. While, in peace time, to become an officer required high quality material, here and now, several brave soldiers were accepted to higher rank only due to their courage in battle. In some cases, it is possible to say that many should not have been promoted.

So, several (fighter) Gruppen were placed under the command of good pilots but very bad leaders. Those men were often unable to psychologically support their men in the extremely difficult situations in which we fought (Allied supremacy was so great that our chances of survival decreased daily, to assume their authority in a clever way, and above all to help their men avoid unnecessary losses in action. On the contrary, often chasing after awards and promotion, the only important thing for them was to claim the maximum number of victories, even if the cost was high in wingmen or inexperienced pilots. Discovering their incapacity in their role, those wartime officers often used a blind authoritarianism, and nearly all of them were alcoholics. I saw them nearly daily drinking at the officers' mess. Some drank an entire bottle of Cognac every day. When some young Leutnant, like me, refused to drink in such an ill-considered manner, he had to withstand constant scoffing. Many of the German aces about whom one hears so much were not such good examples of leadership.

(Lt. Hans Berger, Stk. of 3./JG 1)

Above: After being tested with conventional engines in 1941, the Me 262 made its first flight with turbojet propulsion on 18 July 1942. The jet fighter represented the best hope for the *Jagdwaffe* which was finding itself unable to deal with the large American bomber formations. Created in the summer of 1944, the first experimental combat unit equipped with this revolutionary aircraft proved its capability, and motivated the Luftwaffe to create more such units. One of these was III./EJG 2, placed under the command of the ace Oberstleutnant Heinz Bär (seen here on the wing of a Me 262 at Lechfeld in March 1945).

Above: JV 44 was equipped with Me 262s, and manned by a hand-picked selection of highly-skilled pilots. Even if they were not all renowned aces (as was their leader, General Adolf Galland), they all had extensive combat experience. This was the case with Fw. Franz Steiner (formerly JG 1 and JG 11, with 12 victories), who flew this 'White 5'.

Right: On 25 December 1944, JG 3 was sent in force to counter US bombers over eastern Belgium – and suffered heavy losses. Belgian civilians watch GIs of the 413rd AA Regiment, who are searching for souvenirs in the machine that they have just shot down near Eupen. Bf 109G-10 'Black 7' (WNr. 490708) of 2./JG 3 was manned by Uffz. Franz Mörl who became a POW.
(US National Archives)

Left and below: After operating in Northern France until March 1943, I./NJG 4 moved to Belgium to operate from the new-built Florennes airfield. From there the Bf 110s (and later the Ju 88s) of the Gruppe will encounter British night-bombers flying over southern Belgium. I./NJG 4 was rarely used in day operations (although on 17 August 1943, three or four planes fell, victims of escorting American fighters). At the end of August 1944, I./NJG 4 evacuated to Germany and, in the winter of 1944–45, flew in the Battle of the Bulge. This Ju 88G '3C+FK' of the 2nd Staffel is being readied for an operation over the Ardennes.
(Karl Kern)

141

Left and centre left: If the Me 262 *Schwalbe* is the best-known jet of the Luftwaffe, the Arado 234 *Blitz* is remembered as the first jet bomber. It came too late to take part in the defence of the Normandy beaches, but some were used as recce machines in July 1944. In August 1944, III./KG 76 was the first bomber unit equipped with the new jet, and its 9th Staffel was operational from the beginning of December 1944. From Münster-Handorf, the bombers operated mainly over Belgium in the Battle of the Bulge. On 24 December 1944, led by the Staffelkapitän, Hptm. Dieter Lukesch, nine Arados bombed the main station of the Belgian town of Liège; the first jet bombing raid in history. On Christmas day, two more attacks were launched against Liège. The following days saw actions against Verviers and Bastogne. The Ar 234s were also engaged on *Operation Bodenplatte* and in the *Florian Geyer* attacks against the harbour of Antwerp – already the target of the V weapons. But the *Blitz* was never made in sufficient numbers to make a difference against the almost total Allied air supremacy, and most were shot down by fighters.
(via Chuinard)

Below: In January 1945, JG 53 *Pik-As* remained in southwest Germany to oppose the Western Allies while JG 1, JG 3, JG 4, JG 11 and JG 77 moved to airfields in East Germany and in Poland to try and stop the Soviet advance on Berlin. This Bf 109G-14 'Blue 4' of 12./JG 53, photographed at Kirrlach on 13 January 1945, is warming its engine before take-off. Note the underside of the engine cowling painted in yellow, as well as the radio antenna for the FuG 16ZY under the left wing.

Above: On 1 January 1945, JG 2 was sent over Belgium as part of *Operation Bodenplatte* to attack the St Trond airfield (the base of II./NJG 1 in 1941/1944). In that operation, the *Richthofen* Geschwader lost around 33 pilots, 9 of them becoming POWs. This was the case for Fw. Werner Hohenberg (of the 4th Staffel), his FW 190D-9 'Chevron II' (WNr. 210194) being shot down by AA guns near Aachen. Notice the yellow-white-yellow coloured Defence of the Reich band of the Geschwader. *(US National Archives)*

Above and left: As they roved over European skies, Allied pilots came across some strange aircraft. On 3 February 1945, at 12.30hr, American P-51s of 55 and 343 FG discovered a formation of the unusual *Mistel* composite aircraft near Boizenburg. They may have been from KG 200, flying from Denmark (where they had been assembled for an operation on Scapa Flow) to the south. Five *Mistel* were claimed by the fighters. The first picture shows the pilot of a *Mistel 1* (Bf 109 and Ju 88A-4) baling out at low altitude. The other shows a lone unmanned Ju 88 (abandoned by the *Mistel* pilot) flying for a short time before crashing. *(US National Archives)*

Left: In 1944, a new Luftwaffe weapon appeared. Using old Ju 88 bombers (by now mainly replaced by the Ju 188), the Germans created a composite aircraft known as *Mistel* (mistletoe), also called *Vater und Sohn* or *Hugepack*. A single-engined fighter was attached to the top of the unmanned bomber, with control links between them. The pilot sat in the fighter, although the flight to the target was usually powered by the bomber's engines. As he arrived over the target, the pilot would start the fighter's engines, before aiming the bomber (which was packed with explosives) and releasing it. He returned to base, while the bomber would (it was hoped) crash into the target and destroy it.
(US National Archives)

Right: *Mistel* operations were not a great success, although they were used in the East against the Oder bridges in the last weeks of the war. Many machines were found intact on German airfields, such as the one photographed here in 1945, apparently in Bernburg. It is a *Mistel 2*, formed from a FW 190 and a Ju 88G. *Mistel 1* comprised a Bf 109F and a Ju 88A, while jet-powered *Mistels*, using a Me 262/Ar 234 combination, were considered.
(US National Archives)

Above: Often said to have been obsolete by 1941, the Ju 87 actually flew on all fronts until the end of the war. In 1943, they proved their deadly effectiveness over the Aegean. In the East, fitted with underwing guns, they acted as tankbusters, led by such aces as Oberst Rudel. In the West, they often operated by night in *Störgeschwader*, and were very active around Bastogne in December 1944. US troops captured this train near Hameln, loaded with dismantled Ju 87s. All seem to be in a good state and were perhaps being evacuated to operate further east. *(USAAF)*

Above: On 30 March 1945, this Me 262A-1A in unpainted metal – but wearing its WNr. (111)711 – landed on the airfield of Rhein–Main. The pilot, who had decided to surrender, was Hans Fay. A test-pilot, he had been many years at the Erla Werk VII, established by the Germans on the Deurne airfield, near the Belgian town of Antwerp.
(US National Archives)

Left, below right and below left: **On 11 March 1945 at 15.00hr Lt. Anton Wöffen took off from Hopsten airfield leading 4 Bf 109s from 6./JG 27 for a recce in the Duisburg–Wesel area. While attacking an Auster, the Staffelführer's Bf 109G-10 came under fire from light AA and was hit in the radiator and the fuselage. Wöffen was forced to belly-land 'Yellow 24' west of Rheinberg (near Wesel), and was quickly captured by American soldiers.**

Right: **The Bachem 349 *Natter* was one of those original projects born in the last months of the war, when the German High Command could only place its faith in secret weapons. This tiny rocket-powered machine was designed to be launched vertically when bomber groups overflew its base. Quickly gaining height, the pilot would fire the rockets in the aircraft's nose at the bombers before ejecting his seat and parachute. Only around 30 *Natters* were launched (including eight with pilots).**

Left and below: The swept-wing, rocket-powered Me 163 first flew as an unpowered glider in early 1941. It was planned as a high-performance local interceptor, although with extremely short range. The pilots who manned this unconventional aircraft remember its excellent manoeuvrability, although landings could be dangerous. It had no undercarriage, using instead a detachable wheeled trolley on its take-off run. An extendable skid was all it had to land on, and a heavy landing was enough to detonate any remaining rocket propellant. No other air force had anything to compare with this unusual 'manned missile'.

Left: By the end of the war, He 111s were often transferred to second line units and used as transport machines for high-ranking officers. This ex-bomber (coded 'CM +??') is seen after landing on a Dutch airfield in February 1945. It brought a General of the Fallschirmtruppe (paratroopers) and some supplies (including mail) for the soldiers. Note the black letters outlined in white.
(J-L. Roba)

Above and below: I. and II./JG 1 were the sole Luftwaffe Gruppen equipped with the He 162 *Salamander*. Jet-powered but largely made from wood, it was a last-ditch attempt to produce a simple, cheap, but high-performance fighter. Pilots who flew it remember its speed and manoeuvrability, but structural problems and lack of fuel for pilot training hampered its effectiveness. Both Gruppen moved to Leck in Schleswig-Holstein in anticipation of the surrender and to avoid being captured by the Soviets. Several He 162s were dismantled by the Allies and studied in their home countries, as shown by the one here painted in French markings.

Above: **When British troops captured Wunstorf airfield, near Hanover, they came across this immaculate Ju 88 of the *Nachtjagd*. '3C + PN' (WNr. 620643) belonged to 5./NJG 4, and had the classic late-war camouflage: mottled upper surfaces, pale blue fuselage and undersurfaces. The tail of the other machine on the left has its camouflage obliterating the national markings.**
(IWM)

Below: **At Wunstorf, the British also found some Bf 109G-6s (presumably belonging to training units) with this unusual camouflage.**
(via J-L. Roba)

Right and below: **If there was an award for the most unusual aircraft of the Luftwaffe, no doubt the twin-engined Do 335 fighter would be among the serious candidates. Its history began in 1937 when Dornier presented a patent for a propulsion system including two engines placed on the same axis, one in front pulling, and the other behind, pushing. The resulting fighter had a superb theoretical performance, but problems with vibration and airflow interference from the propellers limited production to only a few.**

Right: **After the German surrender, F/O Fernand Capon from Belgium inspects captured aircraft on Westerland (island of Sylt) airfield. This Me 410A-2 'F4 + EC' was in Seenotgruppe 80, an air-sea rescue unit usually equipped with seaplanes. But with growing Allied airpower, these units received fighters to provide defensive cover over a rescue zone.**
(Fernand Capon)

149

Above: At the end of the war, many German soldiers desperately tried to escape from being captured by the Soviets. Aircraft were loaded with aircrew and ground personnel and flown to the West to surrender to the British and Americans. This Ju 87G which came from Czechoslovakia must have landed around 8 May 1945 on Eschwege airfield (captured by US troops). The pilot on the left is a veteran wearing the *Deutsche Kreuz im Gold* and the Luftwaffe clasp for many combat missions.

Left: Under the wing of this Ju 87G is a Rheinmetall Flak 18 37mm automatic cannon. This weapon was a successful tankbuster, and permitted famous ace Oberst Ulrich Rudel to knock out over 500 tanks on the Eastern Front from 1942 to 1945.
(USAAF)

CHAPTER TWENTY-ONE

Pilot Training

In early 1944, I was transferred to the school fighter squadron 2./JG 107 led by Oblt. Engelberger and established on the airfield of Toul in occupied France. From then on, we operated autonomously, thanks to the several training flights. We learned to fully understand our aircraft. After Toul, our group was transferred to Nancy, a neighbouring airfield (still in French Lorraine) where we hoped to see our training end. We were impatient for our baptism of fire and were much deceived when we were told that we would have to wait several more months to reach the front line. We began instrument flights for blind flying training on NAA 57s, a captured American plane, part of our war booty from June 1940. After ten hours of this training, we began the night flights.

One of these was catastrophic. It was already night when my comrade Krüger and myself started as a pair with our NAA 57s. We made some turns together when flame illuminated the sky. My friend had just been shot down by a Mosquito. Panic invaded me. I changed my course continuously and abruptly, flying risky manoeuvres trying to avoid the Mosquito. In spite of this, I could feel him lurking around me. I remained in the sky as long as I could, not knowing where I was. When I finally decided to land, the enemy was certainly very far on his way home. But the most difficult task was before me: to find my airfield in a dark (inky) night, without radio and being totally lost. I decided to fly at medium height and make large circles, in the hope of passing near my 'home'. On the ground, everything was in darkness, without any clues to help me find my position. After several minutes, when I began to despair, I saw a flash on the ground. My landing strip illuminated for one or two seconds. I knew then the direction I had to fly. I waited anxiously for about 30 seconds for the next light. This time, I was nearby. When the airfield lit up once again, I checked my direction and began to dive. The strip flashed (switched on) a last time just as my wheels touched the ground. I left my aircraft bathed in perspiration.
(Ofhr. Peter Esser)

Above: This Bücker 131 *Jungmann* photographed at Danzig-Langfuhr in mid-1943 belonged to the Sch./FAR 52 *Fliegerausbildungregiment* (Pilot Training Regiment). This school unit had integrated in mid-1943 the FFS A/B 6 *Flugzeugführerschule* (pilot school) A/B certificates for light planes. The insignia carried on the cowling is more elaborate than usual: a red coat of arms with two white crosses and a crown.

Below: Focke-Wulf 44 *Stieglitz* coded 'RN + AE' at Klagenfurt (Austria) during the winter of 1940–41. It wears the insigna of A/B Schule 14. With the He 72, the Kl 35 and the Bü 131, the *Stieglitz* was usually one of the first aircraft flown by budding pilots.

Above: **The high-winged Focke-Wulf 56** *Stösser* **also served in flying schools, often being used for aerobatics training. It was also the first aircraft designed by the famous designer Kurt Tank. 'RT + NR' belonged to FFS A/B 24 and was photographed at Ülmutz. This school moved to Kitzingen/Main in February 1943 before going to Straubing (from June 1943).**

Below: **Quackenbrück, April 1943. This Focke-Wulf 58** *Weihe* **coded 'CM + AS' belongs to A/B 33** *Seerappen.* **The school (named FFS A/B 5 until March 1941) was created at Seerappen in Eastern Prussia and wore the 'Seahorse' badge (***Seerappen*** in German) from then on, even when it moved to Quackenbrück where it was integrated into A/B 33. The FW 58 was generally the first twin-engined machine flown by trainee pilots.**

Right: **Summer 1943. A Bücker 181** *Bestmann* **belonging to FFS A/B 71 based at Prossnitz. This aircraft was much appreciated in Luftwaffe schools: it was comfortable (with side-by-side seating) and manoeuvrable (it was first designed as a sports plane). This aircraft was used by several countries for some years after the war.**

Left: **Arado 96 'CD + OL(?)' of FFS A/B 4 photographed in the Hungarian skies in 1944 (the school was situated at Neudorf/Oppeln). At the end of the B certificate course, students flew this type, their first with retractable landing gear and a variable-pitch airscrew, to see if they had the aptitude for fighter training. Most pilots who flew it have a soft spot for this machine.**

Right: **The Bf 109 had quite difficult flying characteristics (especially the later models) so a two-seater version was developed from the Bf 109G. The Bf 109G-12 first appeared in the** *Jagdschule* **during the spring of 1944.**

Left and below: **After gaining their A/B certificate, pilots chosen for the fighter arm were transferred to *Jagdfliegerschule* (fighter pilots schools) where they usually continued their training on Ar 96s. Some schools also used captured foreign fighters and trainers, such as this North American 57 (monoplane) and Polikarpov I-15 *Chato*, both belonging to the Jagdfliegerschule 3 based at Wien-Schwechat (Austria).**

Left: **The last stage of training for a fighter pilot was the *Ergänzungsjagdgruppe* (complement squadron), a unit where the students were taught by experienced combat pilots. Here they were given final combat-related tuition, and the latest advice on front-line conditions and tactics. It was almost the equivalent of the British OTU. These units also had an *Einsatzstaffel* (combat squadron) in which the instructors could lead the students in their first combat missions. Several victories were claimed by these tiny units. Show here is a Bf 109 of EJG West, based in Southern France (the photo presumably taken in Saint Jean d'Angély).**

Right: When the Wehrmacht entered Czechoslovakia, they found valuable war booty, aircraft as well as tanks. From 1938, the Luftwaffe started to equip a few units with the Avia B-534, but growing Bf 109 production relegated the Czech machines to the trainer role. From 1943, the Avia B-534s (alongside the first models of Ju 87) were transferred to the *Luftlandegeschwader* to tow the gliders (mainly DFS 230s). So this foreign machine began its German career as a front-line fighter, was relegated to a training role, then finally returned to the front as a glider tug. The B-534 shown here was photographed in 1940 at the Herzogenaurach flying school.
(Kühne)

Left: One of the least-known transport planes of the Luftwaffe is the Siebel 204, also used as a liaison and training machine. After the war, the Si 204 was produced in France and Czechoslovakia for their air forces, being made until the mid-1950s. This particular machine belongs to a *Blindflugschule* (blind-flying school) and carries two yellow fuselage bands.

Right: This Ju 88A-12 was photographed in Denmark after a landing gear collapse. It belonged to FFS (B) 34 ('B' for blind), a school based in Copenhagen and designated as Blindflugschule 4 until October 1943. Notice the two yellow fuselage bands and the school's insignia: a jumping bull blinded with a scarf.

Comparisons of Major Ranks

Luftwaffe	USAAF	RAF
Reichsmarschall		
Generalfeldmarschall	General (5-Star)	Marshal of the RAF
Generaloberst	General (4-Star)	Air Chief Marshal
General der Flieger	Lieutenant General	Air Marshal
Generalleutnant	Major General	Air Vice-Marshal
Generalmajor	Brigadier General	Air Commodore
Oberst	Colonel	Group Captain
Oberstleutnant (Obstlt.)	Lieutenant Colonel	Wing Commander
Major	Major	Squadron Leader
Hauptmann (Hptm.)	Captain	Flight Lieutenant
Oberleutnant (Oblt.)	1st Lieutenant	Flying Officer
Leutnant (Lt.)	2nd Lieutenant	Pilot Officer
Stabsfeldwebel (StFw.)	Flight Officer	Warrant Officer
Oberfähnrich (Ofhr.)	–	–
Oberfeldwebel (Ofw.)	Master Sergeant	Flight Sergeant
Fähnrich (Fhr.)	Officer Candidate	–
Feldwebel (Fw.)	Technical Sergeant	Sergeant
Unteroffizier (Uffz.)	Staff Sergeant	Corporal
Obergefreiter (Ogfr.)	Corporal	Leading Aircraftsman
Gefreiter (Gefr.)	Private First Class	Aircraftsman First Class
Flieger (Flg.)	Private Second Class	Aircraftsman Second Class

Glossary

A/B Schule	Flying School
Abschuss	Air claim
Alarmstart	Scramble
Deutsche Kreuz im Gold (DKG)	German Cross in Gold
Eichenlaub (El.)	Knight's Cross with Oak Leaves
Einsatz	Operational Flight
Eisernes Kreuz I, II (EK I, EK II)	Iron Cross (1st and 2nd Class)
Ergänzungsgruppe (EGr.)	Replacement or complement Wing
Flak	A.A. artillery
Führer	Leader
Geschwader	Roughly equivalent to three RAF wings. Comprises three or four Gruppen
Gruppe	Group containing three or four Staffeln. Designated by Roman figures, eg: III./JG 77
Gruppenkommandeur (GK)	'Commander' or 'Captain', a Gruppe command position rather than a rank
Jäger	Fighter
Jagdbomber (Jabo)	Fighter-bomber
Jagdgeschwader (JG)	Fighter wing, includes three or four Gruppen
Jagdwaffe	Fighter Arm or Fighter Force
Kampfgeschwader (KG)	Bomber Wing
Kommodore	'Commodore' or 'Captain', a Geschwader command position rather than a rank
Luftwaffe (LW)	Air Force
Maschine Gewehr (MG)	Machine Gun
Maschine Kanone (MK)	Machine Cannon
Nachtjäger	Nightfighter
Reflex Visier (Revi)	Gunsight
Reichsluftfahrtministerium (RLM)	German Air Ministry
Reichsverteidigung	Air Defence of Germany
Ritterkreuz(träger) (RK/RKT)	Knight's Cross (holder)
Rotte	Tactical element of two aircraft
Rottenflieger	Wingman, the second man in the Rotte
Rottenführer	Leader of an element of two aircraft
Schlachtgeschwader (SG)	Ground attack wing
Schwarm	Flight of four aircraft
Schwarmführer	Flight leader
Schwerten (S)	Knight's Cross with Oak Leaves and Swords

Stab	Staff Flight
Staffel	Roughly equivalent to a Squadron, originally containing twelve aircraft (three Schwärme). Designated sequentially within the Geschwader by arabic figures, eg, 7./JG 2, which is 7 Staffel, the 1st Staffel of the 3rd Gruppe of Jagdgeschwader 2 (before mid-1944).
Staffelkapitän (Stk.)	'Captain', a Staffel command position rather than a rank
Transportgeschwader (TG)	Transport wing
Viermots	Four-engined bombers
Zerstörergeschwader (ZG)	Heavy fighter wing (Bf 110 or Bf 410 twin-engined fighter)
Zweimots	Twin-engined bombers

Selected Reading List

Aders G. and Held W., *Jagdgeschwader 51 'Mölders'*, Motorbuch Verlag, Stuttgart, 1985.

Balke U., *Die Operativen Einsätze des KG 2 im zweiten Weltkrieg*, Bernard und Graefe Verlag, Koblenz, 1989.

Caldwell Donald L., *JG 26 Top Guns of the Luftwaffe*, Orion Books, New-York, 1991.

Dierich Wolfgang, *Die Verbände der Luftwaffe 1935–1945*, Motorbuch Verlag, Stuttgart, 1976.

Freeman R., *The Mighty Eighth War Diary*, London, Janes, 1981.

Girbig W., *Jagdgeschwader 5 'Eismeerjäger'*, Motorbuch Verlag, Stuttgart, 1975.

Marshall F., *Sea Eagles*, Air Research Publ., Walton on Thames, 1993.

Mombeek E., *Reichsverteidigung: Die Geschichte des Jagdgeschwaders 1*, self published, Belgium, 1993.

Obermaier E. *Die Ritterkreuzträger der Luftwaffe 1939/1945 (Band I Jagdflieger)*, Dieter Hoffmann Verlag, Mainz, 1989.

Prien Jochen, *'Pik-As' Geschichte des Jagdgeschwader 53*, self-published, Hamburg, 1991.

Ries K., *Luftwaffen Story*, Dieter Hofmann Verlag, Mainz, 1974.

Ries K., *Deutsch Flugzeugführerschulen und ihre Maschinen*, Motorbuch Verlag, Stuttgart, 1988.

Roba J-L. and Mombeek E., *La Chasse de Jour Allemande en Roumanie*, Ed. Modelism Intern. srl, Bucarest 1994.

Rosch Barry C., *Luftwaffe Codes, Markings & Units 1939–1945*, Schiffer Military/Aviation History, Atglen, 1995.